STEPS TO CHRIST

Study Workbook

Dr. Dennis L. Waters, D. Min.

TEACH Services, Inc.
PUBLISHING
www.TEACHServices.com • (800) 367-1844

World rights reserved. This book or any portion thereof may not be copied or reproduced in any form or manner whatever, except as provided by law, without the written permission of the publisher, except by a reviewer who may quote brief passages in a review.

The author assumes full responsibility for the accuracy of all facts and quotations as cited in this book. The opinions expressed in this book are the author's personal views and interpretations, and do not necessarily reflect those of the publisher.

This book is provided with the understanding that the publisher is not engaged in giving spiritual, legal, medical, or other professional advice. If authoritative advice is needed, the reader should seek the counsel of a competent professional.

Copyright © 2008, 2017 TEACH Services, Inc.
ISBN-13: 978-1-57258-512-6 (Paperback)
Library of Congress Control Number: 2008924404

www.TEACHServices.com • (800) 367-1844

SPECIAL THANKS

The publication of this work for me, represents many years of Christian growth. Additionally, it represents the help of many Christian friends and colleagues. Let me, therefore, take this opportunity to thank God for His saving power, and for His Lordship of my life. Truly "the Blood of Jesus Christ continuously cleanses us from all sin." Next, let me thank my dear devoted wife of 20+ years, Mrs. Hattie Waters, who gave me joy, hope, encouragement, and financial support through the years of developing this project. Thanks to all my children, Dennis Jr., Bobby, Hattie, Tahisha, and Latrece. A special thanks to the members of Truth Tabernacle SDA Church, York, PA; Shiloh SDA Church, Petersburg, VA; Sharon SDA Church, Crewe, VA; Unity SDA Church, Frederick, MD and New Life SDA Church, Gaithersburg, MD.

Especially do I praise God for Sister Barbara Mejia-Mota, who typed this manuscript, for Vikki Fields and Vickie Massenburg, who edited it, and for Ronald Bynum, Mark Brown, Peter Barrow, Pete Palmer, and Yvonne Grigsby who led small groups in the study of this book. Again to Ronald Bynum, my lifelong friend in Christ, and Evelyn his dear wife, thank you for the tremendous spiritual encouragement that God blessed you to give to this project.

FOREWORD

Life's journey is not one embarked upon by choice. For all its travelers, birth becomes a bon voyage party and by simply living, must travel. Each path taken, though well worn, must be blazed anew. Time and social changes constantly alter the terrain and have now caused life's journey to be the source of much pain and fear to many a traveler. But oh, the joy. After many wrong turns, dead ends, stumbles, falls, and skinned knees, the wanderer hears of One who not only has traveled the road before us and successfully completed the trip, but offers to be our guide and companion. The book, STEPS TO CHRIST, leads many to discover the freedom, power, and victory found in a life with Jesus as our Friend and Guide. And now divine inspiration has given us another tool to help us explore this partnership between God and man. Penned by Pastor Dennis L. Waters, the STEPS TO CHRIST Study Workbook highlights key points that signal the reader to pause, appreciate, and admire the beauty and meaning of each. This study deepens your experience, with probing questions that lead you to meditate on and savor God's love, and how it factors into your journey. Having used it to lead a small group study, I have witnessed and personally experienced the depths to which it can lead. I invite you to read this exceptional book, and with this study workbook, strengthen your relationship with Jesus. I pray that your journey, with Him by your side, grows sweeter and sweeter as you get nearer to your glorious destination.

                                              Elder Mark Brown
                                              New Life SDA Church
                                              Gaithersburg, MD

PREFACE

STEPS TO CHRIST outlines in graphic and glorious language the steps, the process, the way, in which a person comes to know Christ, live in Christ, and live with Christ. It is a clear and concise statement of the profound truth in simple form.

Persons the world over have received this classic. Millions are blessed each year as this esteemed volume is read. This study workbook will add to, will multiply your blessedness. By assisting you in exploring the depths of meaning and experience in the things of God, it promises to enrich your life.

Hundreds, yea thousands have benefited from simply reading STEPS TO CHRIST. Here is an opportunity to experience the profound truth of this volume on another level.

To gain the greatest benefit from this study workbook, study a chapter on your own. Then refer to the Appendix for answers by individuals who have completed the study. Pray each time you study, seek a rich experience in the things of God, and then enjoy your journey. Whenever possible sit with a small group of like minded individuals, and under the inspiration of the Holy Spirit compare answers.

". . . They that feared the Lord, spake often one to another: and the Lord hearkened, and heard it, and a book of remembrance was written before him for them that feared the Lord, and that thought upon His name." Malachi 3:16.

INTRODUCTION

This Study Workbook has been "field tested" in different areas and in different ways. To obtain the greatest personal and corporate blessing and benefit from this study, let me suggest methods of use, by recalling three different experiences.

The first and most important methods of study is the foundation for all the rest. This Study Workbook is expecially made for individual private study. The questions are mostly short essay answer type. There are also fill in the blank, multiple choice, and true and false answers. Use the Bible, a dictionary, and of course the book STEPS TO CHRIST. Think through your answers and write them out. The greatest benefits are realized, seen and felt, by those who do this type of study first. This is foundational.

The next method of study is to bring the answers that God, through prayer and study, has given you, and compare your answers with a small group of two, ten or fifteen persons. Following this you can have a discussion of the answers in a church-wide prayer meeting like format.

Finally, as was done in a beautiful way at the New Life SDA Church of Gaithersburg, MD, you can use the book "Steps To Christ" as a theme for a Week of Prayer. The message of this book was dramatically portrayed using art, drama, poetry and prose.

This Study Workbook will bless and benefit your life, whether you are an individual just getting to know Christ, a mature Christian desirous of cooperating with Christ in your spiritual growth, or a more mature Christian who seeks to lead your family and friends to Christ. You will experience a deep sense of satisfaction and joy as you listen to the voice of God speak to you in these pages.

My prayer is that you experience God's presence, see His face, and hear His voice as you study this material, and that you receive the healing benefit from the blessings that come to those who know God.

TABLE OF CONTENTS

Chapter 1 God's Love for Man 1
Chapter 2 The Sinner's Need of Christ 5
Chapter 3 Repentance-Part 1 9
Chapter 4 Repentance-Part 2 15
Chapter 5 Confession 21
Chapter 6 Consecration 25
Chapter 7 Faith and Acceptance 31
Chapter 8 The Test of Discipleship 37
Chapter 9 Growing up Into Christ 43
Chapter 10 The Walk and the Life 49
Chapter 11 A Knowledge of God 55
Chapter 12 The Privilege of Prayer 63
Chapter 13 What to Do With Doubt 69
Chapter 14 Rejoicing in the Lord 75
Appendix - Study Workbook Answers 81

GOD'S LOVE FOR MAN

1. What two things testify of God's love.

   _____
   _____
   _____

2. What do we learn about God from the bird, flowers, and trees?

   _____
   _____
   _____

3. What has God declared about His character in His word?

   _____
   _____

4. Explain the meaning of the statement, "Though all these evidences have been given the enemy of good blinded the minds of men, so that they look upon God with fear; they thought of Him as severe and unforgiving. Satan led men to conceive of God as a being whose chief attribute is stern justice-one who is a severe judge, a harsh, exacting creditor. He pictured the Creator as a being who is watching with jealous eye to discern the errors and mistakes of men, that He may visit judgments upon them."

   _____
   _____
   _____
   _____

CHAPTER 1 - *GOD'S LOVE FOR MAN*

5. Why did Jesus come to live among people?

   _____
   _____
   _____

6. How did Jesus reveal God's love, mercy and compassion?

   _____
   _____
   _____

7. Describe the character of God as it was revealed by Jesus.

   _____
   _____
   _____

8. What was it that broke the heart of the Son of God? Why was this such a traumatic experience for Christ?

   _____
   _____
   _____

9. Did love make God give Jesus to the world or did God begin to love the world when Jesus came to the earth and died? Explain the difference between these two concepts.

   _____
   _____
   _____
   _____

CHAPTER 1 - *GOD'S LOVE FOR MAN*

10. The Bible says, "God so loved the world that He gave His only begotten Son'. What does it mean that God "gave" His Son?

    _____
    _____
    _____

11. Why was this such a great sacrifice?

    _____
    _____
    _____

12. Since God was willing to give so much for us, how should we think of ourselves?

    _____
    _____
    _____

13. Read and answer the following questions. "The more we study the divine character in the light of the cross, the more we see mercy, tenderness and forgiveness blended with equity, and justice and the more clearly we discern innumerable evidences of a love that is infinite. . . . " Describe what we see as we look at the cross. In what way do we see mercy as we look at the cross of Calvary?

    _____
    _____
    _____

14. In what way do we see tenderness as we look at the cross?

    _____
    _____
    _____

CHAPTER 1 - *GOD'S LOVE FOR MAN*

15. In what way do we see forgiveness as we look at the cross?

16. In what way do we see equity as we look at the cross?

17. In what way do we see justice as we look at the cross?

18. Where is God's love most clearly revealed?

THE SINNER'S NEED OF CHRIST

1. Describe man's original condition, including his relationship to God.

   _____
   _____
   _____

2. Describe man's condition after he disobeyed God. What was his relationship to Satan after he disobeyed God? How did disobedience affect his relationship to God?

   _____
   _____
   _____

3. After the fall of Adam, it became possible/impossible (choose one) for us to resist the power of evil and escape from the pit of sin in our own strength.

4. What was Satan's purpose in causing the fall of man? What would he say this evil resulted from?

   _____
   _____
   _____

5. Why would sinners find heaven to be a place of torture, if they were allowed to enter?

   _____
   _____
   _____

CHAPTER 2 - *THE SINNER'S NEED OF CHRIST*

6. What type of heart finds no joy in communion with God?

   _____
   _____

7. Education, culture, the exercise of the will, and human effort may produce an outward correctness of behavior. What is it they cannot do?

   _____
   _____
   _____

8. Whose power works from within to change a person from sin to holiness?

   _____
   _____

9. Being born again means receiving from Christ a new _____, new _____, _____ and _____ leading to a new _____.

10. What does it means to have new desires, purposes and motives?

    _____
    _____
    _____

11. Why is it not enough to simply develop the good which already exist in a person?

    _____
    _____
    _____

CHAPTER 2 - *THE SINNER'S NEED OF CHRIST*

12. In addition to perceiving the loving-kindness of God, the wisdom and fatherly tenderness of God, the justice of His law of love, what else must a person see? Read what the Apostle Paul said about this in Romans 7:14, and state what this means to you.

   _____
   _____
   _____

13. When Paul realized the truth about God and truth about himself, how did he respond? See Romans 7:24 and explain what this means to you.

   _____
   _____
   _____

14. How does God respond to this cry? See John 1:29 and state what this means to you.

   _____
   _____
   _____

15. Experiences in both Jacob's and Nathanael's lives are used to illustrate Christ as the Lamb that takes away the sins of the world. Describe in your own words the desperation of Jacob's situation when he saw the ladder coming down from heaven. See Genesis 27-28:17.

   _____
   _____
   _____

CHAPTER 2 - *THE SINNER'S NEED OF CHRIST*

16. Name five things enlisted in behalf of man's redemption.

    _____
    _____
    _____

17. Which of these five things appeals the most powerfully to you? Why?

    _____
    _____
    _____

18. Name four of the five motives which should encourage us to give the heart's loving service to our Creator and Redeemer,

    _____
    _____
    _____

19. What three things are presented in God's Word to warn us against the service of Satan?

    _____
    _____
    _____

20. Which of these is the strongest warning to you? Why?

    _____
    _____

21. Explain in your own words, why individuals who are sinners by nature need Christ?

    _____
    _____

CHAPTER 3
REPENTANCE-PART 1

1. What is the only way that a person can be just with God, or sinner made righteous?

2. What two things does repentance include?

3. What do you think it means to see sin's sinfulness?

4. What do you think it means to turn away from sin in your heart?

5. Esau, Balaam, Judas Iscariot, and Pharaoh are Bible characters who sorrowed because they had sinned, but their sorrow was not true repentance. Why?

CHAPTER 3 - *REPENTANCE 1*

6. How would a person today lament or sorrow over the suffering or consequences of their sin rather than over the sin itself?

7. Name five things that happen to a person which indicates that his/her repentance is genuine.

8. Why does the conscience need to be quickened? See Ephesians 2:1-5.

9. What happens when the conscience is quickened?

10. What did David see or recognize about his sin?

11. What did he long for? What happened to cause him to lose this? See Isaiah 59:2.

CHAPTER 3 - *REPENTANCE 1*

12. Is it within man's power to repent on his own? Explain your answer.
    _____
    _____

13. Who has God exalted to give repentance and forgiveness of sins to us? See Acts 5:31, 32.
    _____
    _____

14. Can we repent without the Spirit of Christ? What then must we do to receive repentance? See Matthew 11:28.
    _____
    _____
    _____

15. How can you know when the Spirit of God is working with you or with others to bring us to repentance?
    _____
    _____
    _____

16. What is it that leads us to repentance? See Romans 2:4. What does this verse mean?
    _____
    _____

17. What must the sinner behold before his heart is softened, his mind impressed, or contrition is inspired in his soul?
    _____
    _____
    _____

CHAPTER 3 - *REPENTANCE 1*

18. How can we reveal Christ as the Saviour dying for the world? Is this simply a matter of telling someone that Christ died for the world?

    _____
    _____
    _____

19. When only will a person apply the above answer to him/her self?

    _____
    _____
    _____

20. Do people always recognize that Christ is drawing them to Himself?

    _____
    _____
    _____

21. How can we recognize this drawing of Christ?

    _____
    _____
    _____

22. What will happen to a person who does not resist Christ's drawing?

    _____
    _____
    _____

CHAPTER 3 - *REPENTANCE 1*

23. What will lead the sinner to the foot of the cross?

24. What is the meaning of this paragraph, "The same divine mind that is working upon the things of nature is speaking to the hearts of men, and creating an inexpressible craving for something they have not. The things of the world cannot satisfy their longing. The Spirit of God is pleading with them to seek for those things that alone can give peace and rest - the grace of Christ, the joy of holiness. Through influences seen and unseen, our Saviour is constantly at work to attract the minds of men from the unsatisfying pleasures of sin to the infinite blessings that may be theirs in Him. To all these souls, who are vainly seeking to drink from the broken cisterns of this world, the divine message is addressed, 'Let him that is athirst come, and whosoever will, let him take the water of life freely.' "

25. How can you and I recognize when we or our friends and relatives are seeking, and/or craving, for something we do not possess?

REPENTANCE-PART 2

1. "We may have flattered ourselves, as did Nicodemus, that our life has been upright, that our moral character is correct, and think that we need not humble the heart before God, like that common sinner: but when the light from Christ shines into our souls, we shall see how impure we are; we shall discern the selfishness of motive, the enmity against God, that has defiled every act of life."

2. What do you think is "the light from Christ which shines in our souls"?

   _____
   _____
   _____

3. When light from Christ shines in our hearts, what four things will we discern about ourselves?

   _____
   _____
   _____
   _____

4. "The soul thus touched will hate its selfishness, abhor its self-love, and will seek, through Christ's righteousness, for the purity of heart that is in harmony with the law of God and the character of Christ." What does this statement mean?

   _____
   _____
   _____
   _____

CHAPTER 4 - *REPENTANCE 2*

5. Are there any small sins in the sight of God?

   _____
   _____
   _____

6. Which sins are especially offensive to God? Why are these sins especially offensive to God?

   _____
   _____
   _____

7. Since pride feels no need of the grace of Christ, what does it do?

   _____
   _____
   _____

8. Use your own words to describe the difference between the publican and the Pharisee of Luke 18:9-13.

   _____
   _____
   _____

9. If you see your sinfulness, where only can you find help?

   _____
   _____
   _____

CHAPTER 4 - *REPENTANCE 2*

10. If an individual feels just a little sinful should he/she wait for stronger persuasions, for better opportunities or for holier tempers? Why or why not?

    _____
    _____
    _____

11. List the reasons Christ took upon Himself the guilt of the disobedient and suffered in the sinner's stead?

    _____
    _____
    _____
    _____

12. What testifies to the terrible enormity of sin and declares that there is no escape from its power, and no hope of a higher life, except through the submission of the soul to Christ? How does it do this?

    _____
    _____
    _____

13. Many times new Christians justify and excuse their sinful actions and attitudes by what they see and hear of Christians. Is this practice acceptable? Explain your answer.

    _____
    _____
    _____

14. Why is the non-Christian's sin greater than the Christian's?

    _____
    _____

CHAPTER 4 - *REPENTANCE 2*

15. Give some reasons why you think that as soon as you recognize that you are sinner you should repent?

    _____

    _____

    _____

16. Name five ways every neglect or rejection of the grace of Christ reacts on an individual?

    _____

    _____

    _____

17. What might hinder a person from changing his or her course of evil any time he or she wants to?

    _____

    _____

    _____

18. When is Christ ready to set us free from sin?

    _____

    _____

19. "Search me, O God, and know my heart: try me and know my thoughts; and see if there be any wicked way in me, and lead me in the way everlasting." Psalms 139: 23. What does this mean?

    _____

    _____

    _____

    _____

CHAPTER 4 - *REPENTANCE 2*

20. What is the difference between true religion and an intellectual religion?

    _____
    _____
    _____

21. Since Christ is the only One who gives us true religion, what should your prayer to Him be?

    _____
    _____

22. What will prayerful study of God's word do for you?

    _____
    _____

23. When you study the Word of God and see the enormity of your sin, should you give up in despair? Why or why not?

    _____
    _____
    _____

24. What inspired all of God's promises and warnings?

    _____
    _____

25. When Satan tells us that we are great sinners what should we do?

    _____
    _____
    _____

CHAPTER 4 - *REPENTANCE 2*

26. When will we best realize the sinfulness of sin? What difference should this make in our lives?

   _____

   _____

   _____

CONFESSION

1. Describe the conditions of obtaining the mercy of God? What must you do to receive His mercy?

   _____
   _____
   _____

2. What is the difference between a fault and a sin? Who should faults be confessed to? Who should sins confessed to?

   _____
   _____
   _____
   _____

3. When you offend your friend or neighbor what should you do first? Then what?

   _____
   _____
   _____

4. Why should you seek the forgiveness of God when you have "only" wronged another human being?

   _____
   _____
   _____

CHAPTER 5 - *CONFESSION*

5. What is the first condition of acceptance?

   _____
   _____
   _____

6. What is the only reason we do not have remission of sins that are past?

   _____
   _____

7. Using the book "Steps To Christ" fill in the blank. " _____ ____ _____, whether _____ or _____, should be _____, and freely _____. It is not to be urged from the sinner. It is _____ to be _____ in a _____ and _____ way, or _____ from those who have no realizing sense of the _____ _____ of _____."

8. What does the following statement mean? "True confession is always of a specific character, and acknowledges particular sins."

   _____
   _____
   _____

9. What is your understanding of the following two statements? "God is ready and willing to forgive every particular sin that you have confessed." and "I have only received the forgiveness of God for the particular sins I have confessed."

   _____
   _____
   _____

CHAPTER 5 - *CONFESSION*

10. What is the result of genuine sorrow for sin?

11. Explain the following statement. "When sin has deadened the moral perception, the wrongdoer does not discern the defects of his character nor realize the enormity of the evil he has committed; and unless he yields to the convicting power of the Holy Spirit, he remains in partial blindness to his sin. His confessions are not sincere and in earnest. To every acknowledgment of his guilt he adds an apology in excuse of his course, declaring that if it had not been for certain circumstances he would not have done this or that, for which he is reproved."

12. What will true repentance lead a person to do?

13. What happens to those persons who acknowledge their guilt? How does this happen?

14. Describe how the Apostle Paul confessed his sin?

CHAPTER 5 - *CONFESSION*

15. What two things will the humble and broken heart subdued by genuine repentance appreciate?

_____

_____

_____

CONSECRATION

1. Look up the word "Consecration" in a dictionary. Write out the definition of this word.

   _____
   _____
   _____

2. What is meant by; "all the heart, or the whole heart being yielded to God"? Why is this necessary?

   _____
   _____
   _____

3. What is the end result of the change that is wrought in us when we yield our whole heart to God?

   _____
   _____
   _____

4. What is the greatest battle ever fought? Explain this.

   _____
   _____
   _____
   _____

CHAPTER 6 - *CONSECRATION*

5. How do you think a person surrenders their will or submits their soul to God?

   _____
   _____
   _____

6. What is blind submission?

   _____
   _____
   _____

7. What is meant by a "mere automaton"?

   _____
   _____
   _____

8. If God forced our submission to Him what would be prevented? Why is this important?

   _____
   _____
   _____

9. Since God will not force our submission to Him, nor will He accept blind submission, nor will He control us without our being able to think, what does He appeal to, to get us to understand Him and ourselves? Why is this important?

   _____
   _____
   _____

CHAPTER 6 - *CONSECRATION*

10. Even though God invites us to give ourselves to Him, what must we do?
    _____
    _____

11. What things draw the heart away from God?
    _____
    _____
    _____

12. Describe the religion that is worth nothing.
    _____
    _____
    _____

13. What is the aim of those who love Christ?
    _____
    _____
    _____

14. If you feel your giving all to God is too great a sacrifice, what should you do?
    _____
    _____
    _____

15. When you give your sin polluted heart to Jesus Christ, what does He do with it? How does He do this?
    _____
    _____

CHAPTER 6 - *CONSECRATION*

16. When are you doing the greatest injury to yourself?

17. What does the following statement mean to you? "No real joy can be found in the path forbidden by Him who knows what is best and who plans for the good of His creatures. The path of transgression is the path of misery and destruction."

18. Is God pleased to see His children suffer?

19. When we give ourselves to Christ, what will He impart to us?

20. When you desire to give yourself to God, but are weak in moral power, in slavery to doubt, controlled by the habits of your life of sin, have made and broken many promises to yourself and to others, unable to control your thoughts, impulses and affections, what can you do to give yourself to Christ?

21. What is the governing power in the nature of man? What is meant by the governing power?

CHAPTER 6 - *CONSECRATION*

22. What will God do when you give your will to Him?

    _____

    _____

23. Is it possible for you to be lost while hoping and desiring to be a Christian? Explain your answer.

    _____

    _____

    _____

24. How can an entire change be made in your life?

    _____

    _____

25. Since God will give you strength to hold stedfast and to live the new life of faith, when you yield yourself to Him, will you today, choose, or will, to give Him your whole heart?

    _____

    _____

FAITH AND ACCEPTANCE

1. Read John 16:8-11. One of the works of the Holy Spirit is to convict of sin. What specifically will you see or be convicted of when the Holy Spirit has quickened your conscience?

2. How will you feel about your motives, heart, and your life altogether?

3. How only can we receive heaven's forgiveness, peace and love in the soul?

4. What does the following mean, "Come now, let us reason together. . ."? How can a person reason with God? Isaiah 1:18.

CHAPTER 7 - *FAITH AND ACCEPTANCE*

5. What does the Lord Jesus Christ mean when He says, "...Though your sins be as scarlet, they shall be white as snow; though they be red like crimson, they shall be as wool"?

   _____
   _____
   _____

6. What three steps do you take to Christ before asking Him to wash away your sins and give you a new heart?

   _____
   _____
   _____

7. Why should you believe Jesus Christ forgives and washes away your sin and gives you a new heart?

   _____
   _____
   _____

8. Write out and repeat aloud the promise of Ezekiel 36:26.

   _____
   _____
   _____
   _____

9. What must you do to receive what God promises?

   _____
   _____

CHAPTER 7 - *FAITH AND ACCEPTANCE*

10. Why did Christ heal diseases and help people with things of this natural world?

    _____

    _____

    _____

11. The paralytic of Bethesda was paralyzed for 38 years. Jesus bade him, "Rise, take up your bed and walk." What two things did he <u>do</u> in response to Christ words?

    _____

    _____

    _____

12. Who gave him the power to walk, after he acted on the word of Christ?

    _____

    _____

    _____

13. How does the condition of a sinner resemble that of the paralyzed man of Bethesda?

    _____

    _____

    _____

    _____

14. In addition to believing God's promises to forgive all of our past sins and to change our hearts, what three things must we do?

    _____

    _____

    _____

CHAPTER 7 - *FAITH AND ACCEPTANCE*

15. If you do not "feel" that you are forgiven and made whole, what should you do?

   _____
   _____
   _____

16. True/False (circle one) God will forgive you and cleanse you from sin, adopt you into His family, and give you power to live a holy life?

   _____
   _____

17. In addition to asking for, and believing that you receive these blessings, what must you do?

   _____
   _____

18. What does Romans 8:1 mean to you?

   _____
   _____
   _____

19. Henceforth you are not your own, you are bought with a price, "Ye were not redeemed with corruptible things, as silver and gold; but with the precious blood of Christ, as of a lamb without blemish and with spot." 1 Peter 1:18, 19. What does this statement mean to you?

   _____
   _____
   _____
   _____

CHAPTER 7 - *FAITH AND ACCEPTANCE*

20. After you have given yourself to Christ the first time, what should you say every day?

    _____
    _____
    _____

21. What should you ask Him every day?

    _____
    _____
    _____

22. How do you remain with Jesus Christ?

    _____
    _____
    _____

23. When can you claim the blessing of forgiveness and cleansing?

    _____
    _____

24. Fill in the blanks. "We may come with all our _____, our _____, our _____, and fall at His feet in _____. It is His _____ to _____us in the arms of His love and to ____ ____our _____, to _____us from all _____."

25. Who are God's promises meant for?

    _____
    _____
    _____

CHAPTER 7 - *FAITH AND ACCEPTANCE*

26. Rather than give ear to the tempter what should we say?

    _____

    _____

    _____

27. What can hurt your soul the most?

    _____

    _____

    _____

28. As we draw near to Christ with confession and repentance what will He do?

    _____

    _____

    _____

A TEST OF DISCIPLESHIP

The first six questions of this chapter are thought questions. As such, they can and should be answered before you read the chapter and after you read the chapter. See if the answers you give before reading and the answers that you give after reading are the same, similar, or completely different.

1. What is being tested in a test of discipleship?

2. Is this a test to see if a person is a disciple?

3. What difference would it make to a person who says, "I am a disciple" and after taking the test found out that they were not a true disciple? What if by taking the test, the person found out they were a true disciple?

CHAPTER 8 - *A TEST OF DISCIPLESHIP*

4. What difference does it make that we take the test now and not later, say at the coming of the Lord Jesus Christ?

   _____
   _____
   _____

5. One of the ways of looking at a test is to consider a test as a metering device. Like the gas gauge in a car, it is a gauge to inform you of how much reserve you have. It gives you a measurement of how much you have of what you need. In this case what is being measured is your relationship with Jesus and your love for Him. This test will reveal therefore your fullness or your emptiness in this relationship. What do you think of the above statements about a test?

   _____
   _____
   _____

6. Another purpose of a test is to help new things to become part of our being, living, and doing. If this is true, then what things would the test of discipleship help to become a part of our being, living, and doing?

   _____
   _____
   _____

7. Can we trust outward signs (shouting, speaking in tongues, etc.), as indicators of our conversions? Why or why not?

   _____
   _____
   _____
   _____

CHAPTER 8 - *A TEST OF DISCIPLESHIP*

8. What are the true indicators of conversion?

   _____
   _____
   _____

9. When we belong to Christ what changes are made in our thought processes and in our goals?

   _____
   _____
   _____

10. What two items are untrustworthy to reveal our new birth?

    _____
    _____

11. In what areas of our life will the new birth become visible?

    _____
    _____
    _____

12. Is repentance possible without reformation? Why or why not?

    _____
    _____

13. Discuss duty becoming a delight?

    _____
    _____
    _____

CHAPTER 8 - *A TEST OF DISCIPLESHIP*

14. What two errors are made by individuals who claim to follow Christ?

   _____
   _____
   _____

15. What is the true sign of discipleship?

   _____
   _____
   _____

16. What motivates our obedience to Christ?

   _____
   _____
   _____

17. What happens to us the closer we come to Christ? What effect do you think this will have upon the person who is coming to Christ?

   _____
   _____
   _____

18. Can you always tell the exact time or place that your conversion took place?

   _____
   _____
   _____

CHAPTER 8 - *A TEST OF DISCIPLESHIP*

19. Will "works" alone get us into heaven?

   _____

   _____

   _____

20. Is it enough to believe in God? Explain your answer.

   _____

   _____

   _____

   _____

   _____

GROWING UP INTO CHRIST

1. Why is it necessary for us to be born again?

   _____
   _____
   _____

2. How much growth is produced in plants by the plants' own care, anxiety and effort?

   _____
   _____

3. What are the gifts in nature that a plant receives to grow?

   _____
   _____

4. Explain the point made in comparing the gifts received by the plants and the growth produced in them, with the Gift of the spiritual life and the growth produced?

   _____
   _____
   _____

5. Define grace and atmosphere using a dictionary. Now explain the statement "God has encircled the world with an atmosphere of grace as real as the air which circulates around the globe."

   _____
   _____
   _____

CHAPTER 9 - *GROWING UP INTO CHRIST*

6. Discuss the following statement. "You are just as dependent upon Christ, in order to live a holy life, as is the branch upon the parent stock for growth and fruitfulness. Apart from Him you have no life. You have no power to resist temptation or to grow in grace and holiness. Abiding in Him, you may flourish. Drawing your life from Him, you will not wither nor be fruitless. You will be like a tree planted by the rivers of water."

   _____
   _____
   _____

7. What does growth in grace, our joy and our usefulness depend on?

   _____
   _____
   _____

8. What are we to give to Christ?

   _____
   _____
   _____

9. What are we to receive or take from Him?

   _____
   _____

10. What should you say and what should you do each morning to consecrate, or devote yourself to God for that day?

    _____
    _____
    _____

CHAPTER 9 - *GROWING UP INTO CHRIST*

11. What should our minds dwell upon?

   _____
   _____
   _____

12. Instead of looking to yourself or letting your mind dwell upon yourself, what should you do?

   _____
   _____
   _____

13. What about Christ should we think and meditate on?

   _____
   _____
   _____

14. How are we transformed into Christ's image?

   _____
   _____
   _____

15. Explain the following statement. "This rest is not found in inactivity, for in the Savior's invitation the promise of rest is united with the call to labor: 'Take my yoke upon you . . . and ye shall find rest.' The heart that rest most fully upon Christ will be the most earnest and active in labor for Him.' "

   _____
   _____
   _____

CHAPTER 9 - *GROWING UP INTO CHRIST*

16. List four things that Satan seeks to divert our minds to, so that we will not meditate on Christ.

    _____

    _____

    _____

17. What happens to people who make themselves the center and who indulge anxiety and fear regarding whether they will be saved?

    _____

    _____

18. What did the Apostle Paul say and live out in his life to dismiss his fear about this?

    _____

    _____

19. What only can break Christ's tie or union with you?

    _____

    _____

20. True or False: We are always free to choose the master we will serve.

    _____

    _____

21. What do you think of the following statements. "The only power that can separate us from God is our power of choice." And "When we choose to stay with God no power can separate us from Him."

    _____

    _____

    _____

CHAPTER 9 - *GROWING UP INTO CHRIST*

22. How are we to behold Christ? And what happens as a result of beholding Him?

    _____

    _____

    _____

23. What traits of character were found in John the disciple when he first came in contact with Christ?

    _____

    _____

    _____

24. What traits of character did he find in Jesus Christ?

    _____

    _____

25. What transformed John?

    _____

    _____

26. "When Christ ascended to heaven the sense of His presence was still with His followers. It was a personal presence, full of love and light." What is the meaning of "personal presence"?

    _____

    _____

    _____

    _____

CHAPTER 9 - *GROWING UP INTO CHRIST*

27. What did the disciples know even though Christ had gone to heaven?

    _____

    _____

28. What makes the union of Christ with His people closer now than when He was on earth?

    _____

    _____

29. After reading this chapter, if a person asked you "How do you grow up into Christ?" or "How do you abide in Christ?" How would you answer?

    _____

    _____

    _____

THE WORK AND THE LIFE

1. Where the life of God is in the hearts of men, what will flow out to others?

2. What is the joy of sinless angels?

3. What is it that selfish hearts regard as humiliating?

4. Describe the spirit that Christ's followers will possess? What is the work Christ's followers will do?

5. How will love to Jesus be manifested?

CHAPTER 10 - *THE WORK AND THE LIFE*

6. For what reason did Christ toil with persistent, earnest, untiring effort?

   _____
   _____

7. Fill in the blanks. "From the _____ to _____, He followed the path of _____ _and sought not to be _____ from arduous tasks, painful travels and exhausting care and labor. He said, 'The Son of man came not to be _____, but to minister and to ___ ____ ____ a ransom for many.' Matthew 20:28. This was the object of His life. Everything else was ___ and _____."

   _____
   _____
   _____
   _____

8. What will those who are partakers of the grace of Christ be ready to make?

   _____
   _____
   _____

9. When a person is born again what also is born in their heart?

   _____
   _____

10. What do you think are the attractions of Christ and the unseen realities of the world to come, that those who are born again will seek to present to others?

    _____
    _____
    _____

CHAPTER 10 - *THE WORK AND THE LIFE*

11. What was God's purpose in giving us a part to act in the plan of redemption? How do you see this plan as being carried out in your life?

    _____

    _____

    _____

12. What is the highest honor, the greatest joy, that is possible for God to bestow upon men?

    _____

    _____

    _____

13. Who are the ones who are brought nearest to the Creator?

    _____

    _____

    _____

14. Why did God choose to make us co-workers with Himself, with Christ, and with the angels?

    _____

    _____

    _____

15. How do you think fellowship with Christ in His suffering, brings us into sympathy with Him?

    _____

    _____

    _____

CHAPTER 10 - *THE WORK AND THE LIFE*

16. What will the encountering of opposition and trial do for you?

17. What will the spirit of unselfish labor for others give you? How do you labor unselfishly for others?

18. What is the only way to grow in grace?

19. What is the meaning of the following statement? "Those who endeavor to maintain Christian life by passively accepting the blessings that come through the means of grace, and doing nothing for Christ, are simply trying to live by eating without working."

20. What happens to the Christian who will not exercise his God given powers in the winning of souls for Christ?

CHAPTER 10 - *THE WORK AND THE LIFE*

21. How can we can sustain the proclamation of the Gospel in heathen lands when we can not go there to personally engage in the work?

    _____

    _____

22. Where can we work for Christ when we cannot go to heathen lands?

    _____

    _____

    _____

23. In addition to healing the sick, and walking upon the storm tossed waves, where else did Christ fulfill His mission? Why is it important for you to know this?

    _____

    _____

    _____

24. Why have many excused themselves from rendering their gifts to the service of Christ?

    _____

    _____

    _____

25. What are we fitting ourselves for by being workers together with God in this life?

    _____

    _____

    _____

A KNOWLEDGE OF GOD

1. Name five things in nature that speak to the open heart and the listening ear, inviting you to become acquainted with the Creator of all things.

   _____
   _____
   _____

2. Why did the Savior link the words of truth of His precious lessons with the trees, birds, flowers, hills, lakes, the beautiful heavens and the incidents and surroundings of daily life?

   _____
   _____
   _____

3. What type of beauty does God love above that which is outwardly attractive?

   _____
   _____

4. What are the quiet graces of the flowers that God would have us cultivate?

   _____
   _____

5. What lessons about God can we learn from the stars in their appointed paths?

   _____
   _____
   _____

CHAPTER 11 - *A KNOWLEDGE OF GOD*

6. How much of God's created universe does He care for and sustain? How do you see Him doing this? Why is it important for us to know that God cares for the universe?

   _____
   _____
   _____

7. What is it that we need to believe about God, which when believed will help us to enjoy a rest of soul to which many have long been strangers?

   _____
   _____
   _____

8. While we are delighting in the beautiful things of this earth, what should we think about?

   _____
   _____
   _____

9. Why is it that the Christian can enjoy the beauty of the earth with even higher appreciation than the poet and naturalist?

   _____
   _____
   _____
   _____

CHAPTER 11 - *A KNOWLEDGE OF GOD*

10. What is the meaning of "His providential workings" in the following statement? "God speaks to us through His providential workings and through the influence of His Spirit upon the heart." Also how are you able to detect God's speaking to you in or by His providential workings?

    _____
    _____
    _____
    _____

11. Read the story of David's first child by Bathsheba in 2 Sam. 12:15-22. What can be said about David's prayer and God's providential workings?

    _____
    _____
    _____
    _____

12. What three things are revealed about God in His Word more clearly than those seen in nature and His providential workings?

    _____
    _____
    _____

13. In what ways are we benefited from a study of the lives of the patriarchs and prophets of the Bible?

    _____
    _____
    _____
    _____

CHAPTER 11 - *A KNOWLEDGE OF GOD*

14. Who is really the One who is being revealed in the whole Bible?

    _____
    _____
    _____

15. How do you think a person fills their whole heart with the Word of God?

    _____
    _____

16. What does meditating on the words of God do for us?

    _____
    _____
    _____

17. What is the subject that angels desire to understand better and which will be the science and the song of the redeemed forever?

    _____
    _____
    _____

18. Name three things which will happen to us as we study and meditate upon the themes of the infinite mercy and the love of Jesus, the sacrifice made in our behalf, the character of our dear Redeemer and Intercessor, and His mission to save His people from their sins?

    _____
    _____
    _____
    _____

CHAPTER 11 - *A KNOWLEDGE OF GOD*

19. When we meditate upon the perfections of Christ's character what will be our desire?

   _____

   _____

   _____

20. What two things will happen to us the more our thoughts are on Christ?

   _____

   _____

   _____

21. Who are the only individuals who will mistake and lose their way when they study the Bible?

   _____

   _____

   _____

22. Summarize in your own words the idea that is communicated by the following paragraph.

   "We should not take the testimony of any man as to what the scriptures teach but should study the words of God for ourselves. If we allow others to do our thinking, we shall have crippled energies and contracted abilities. The noble power of the mind may be so dwarfed by lack of exercise on themes worthy of their concentration as to lose their ability to grasp the deep meaning of the Word of God. The mind will enlarge if it is employed in tracing out the relation of the subjects of the Bible, comparing scripture and spiritual things with spiritual."

   _____

   _____

   _____

CHAPTER 11 - *A KNOWLEDGE OF GOD*

23. What are three benefits that a person will derive from a faithful study of Bible?

   _____

   _____

   _____

24. When you study the Bible, even one passage of the Bible, what two things are you seeking to understand?

   _____

   _____

   _____

25. List times when you could study the Bible if you kept a copy of it with you?

   1. _____ 2. _____ 3. _____

   4. _____ 5. _____ 6. _____

   7. _____ 8. _____ 9. _____

26. What should we ask in prayer before we even open the Bible? Why should we do this?

   _____

   _____

   _____

27. What specifically does the Holy Spirit do for us as we study the Bible?

   _____

   _____

   _____

CHAPTER 11 - *A KNOWLEDGE OF GOD*

28. In the statement which follows, what is the meaning of "effectual teacher"? "The Spirit of Truth is the only effectual teacher of divine truth."

_____

_____

_____

THE PRIVILEGE OF PRAYER

1. In order to commune with God, what must we talk with Him about?

   _____
   _____
   _____

2. In what way do you think prayer enables us to receive God and brings us up to Him?

   _____
   _____
   _____

3. Jesus taught His disciples to pray, what two things did He specifically tell them to present to the Father?

   _____
   _____

4. What made prayer a necessity for our sinless Savior Jesus Christ?

   _____
   _____
   _____

5. What is God waiting to bestow on the ones who will pray to Him?

   _____
   _____
   _____

CHAPTER 12 - *THE PRIVILEGE OF PRAYER*

6. Since prayer does not change God, nor does it inform Him of something He does not know, why is He waiting until we pray before He bestows on us the fullness of His blessings?

   _____
   _____
   _____

7. What happens to individuals who neglect to pray? What are some things that might hinder you from taking time to pray? How do you find time to pray in spite of these things?

   _____
   _____
   _____

8. Name four conditions of answered prayer found in this chapter?

   _____
   _____
   _____

9. What is our work in complying with the condition of not regarding iniquity in our hearts?

   _____
   _____

10. What does it mean to take God at His word?

    _____
    _____
    _____

CHAPTER 12 - *THE PRIVILEGE OF PRAYER*

11. Why is it that we sometimes ask for things which would not be a blessing to us?

12. What should we do when our prayers are not answered?

13. What will happen to us if we take counsel with doubts and fears or try to solve everything that we cannot see clearly before we have faith?

14. How are we to come to God?

15. What does it mean to have a spirit of love and forgiveness in our hearts when we pray?

16. What does it mean to forgive others in the "same manner" and to the "same extent" as we hope to be forgiven? What was/is the manner of Christ's forgiveness to you? What is the extent of that same forgiveness?

CHAPTER 12 - *THE PRIVILEGE OF PRAYER*

17. What must we do if we would grow in faith and experience? Why do you think this is true?

　_____
　_____
　_____

18. Where will individuals who are seeking communion with God be seen?

　_____
　_____

19. Name three kinds of prayer or places of prayer?

　_____
　_____

20. Which one should we insure ourselves against neglecting?

　_____

21. In the following statement, what is meant by "thus stayed on God"? "Satan cannot overcome him whose heart is thus stayed on God."

　_____
　_____

22. Name the time and place when it is inappropriate to pray to God?

　_____
　_____

23. What are some of the things that we should keep before God?

　_____
　_____

CHAPTER 12 - *THE PRIVILEGE OF PRAYER*

24. Is there anything in our lives too dark or nasty for us to pray to God about?

25. What does it mean to pray in Jesus' name?

26. What happens to the person that does nothing but pray?

27. What happens to individuals who take themselves out of the social life, away from the sphere of Christian duty and cross bearing, or cease to work earnestly for the Master?

28. What do we lose when "we neglect the privilege of associating together to strengthen and encourage one another in the service of God"?

29. What does the proper cultivation of the social elements in our nature do for us?

CHAPTER 12 - *THE PRIVILEGE OF PRAYER*

30. How do you properly cultivate the social elements in your nature?

31. What should Christians talk of when associating together? What happens when we do this?

32. Why do we talk of temporal or temporary things? What are some temporal things that we talk of?

33. Why do we talk of our friends? Why do we talk of God?

34. In addition to asking and receiving what should our devotional exercise consist of?

35. How should things be done for the Lord Jesus Christ?

WHAT TO DO WITH DOUBT

1. Define skepticism? What are suggestions of skepticism? Who are the individuals who are especially troubled by suggestions of skepticism?

2. How does Satan seek to use the many things in scripture that cannot be explained or even understood?

3. How could the following questions be asked in another way? "How shall I know the right way? and "If the Bible is indeed the Word of God, how can I be freed from these doubts and perplexities?

4. The evidence that establishes the foundation for our belief in the existence of God, the character of God and the truthfulness of His Word, are established by testimony that appeals to what?

CHAPTER 13 - *WHAT TO DO WITH DOUBT*

5. "It is impossible for finite minds fully to comprehend the character or the works of the Infinite One." In the preceding statement what is the meaning of "finite minds"?

   _____

   _____

   _____

6. From God's dealing with us and motives by which He is moved to act, what may we understand or discern about God?

   _____

   _____

   _____

7. God lets us know as much of His purposes as it is for our good to know, what must we do about that which we cannot or do not know?

   _____

   _____

   _____

8. What are four subjects presented in the Word of God, which have mysteries too deep for the human mind to explain or fully comprehend?

   _____

   _____

   _____

9. Name some subjects or things in today's complex society, which we work with or use everyday which we do not totally understand?

   _____

   _____

   _____

CHAPTER 13 - *WHAT TO DO WITH DOUBT*

10. Where does the difficulty really lie in our inability to understand the mysteries of the natural world and those in the spiritual world?

    _____
    _____
    _____

11. Should we doubt God's Word because we cannot understand everything in it? Why or why not?

    _____
    _____
    _____

12. The fact that God's word cannot be fully understood or comprehended by us should speak to us of its divine authority. Do you agree with this statement? Why or why not?

    _____
    _____
    _____

13. The Bible was written to meet the need and longings of every human heart. What things in the Bible can be discerned or understood by both the highly cultivated mind and by those who are humble and uncultured?

    _____
    _____
    _____

14. What will eventually happen to the reasoning of the sincere seeker for truth if he continues to study the Word of God?

    _____
    _____

CHAPTER 13 - *WHAT TO DO WITH DOUBT*

15. What do we admit when we admit that we cannot understand everything in the Bible?

16. How does Satan work to pervert the investigative powers of the mind as we study the Bible?

17. Should God's Word be charged, when theories and doctrine contrary to the tenor of inspiration, are taught by individuals who claim to get the theories from God's Word? Who should be blamed for this?

18. If we could understand fully God and His works what would happen to our view of God?

19. State the only way that we can obtain an understanding of God's Word?

20. What will the study of the Bible do for us?

CHAPTER 13 - *WHAT TO DO WITH DOUBT*

21. Why should we not deify reason or make a god out of reason? How would a person deify reason or make a god out of reason?

    _____
    _____
    _____

22. Opening God's Word should inspire us with the same reverence and humility as. . . .

    _____
    _____

23. Under what conditions is it possible for skepticism to strengthen in the study of the Bible?

    _____
    _____
    _____

24. When is it not safe to trust individuals explanation of the scriptures?

    _____
    _____
    _____

25. What is the real cause of doubt and skepticism in most cases?

    _____
    _____

26. To which heart are the teachings and restrictions of God's Word not welcomed?

    _____
    _____

CHAPTER 13 - *WHAT TO DO WITH DOUBT*

27. What two things are required to arrive at the Truth found in God's Word?

   _____
   _____

28. What does it mean to "give heed to the light that already shines upon you"? What will happen if you do this?

   _____
   _____

29. What is the evidence that is opened to both the highly educated and the illiterate?

   _____
   _____

30. How do you think a person proves the promises of God's Word?

   _____
   _____
   _____

31. With the things which we cannot understand now, or even after we have studied the Bible, what should we by faith in God do?

   _____
   _____
   _____

32. When will many things which we cannot understand now be explained to us?

   _____
   _____
   _____

REJOICING IN THE LORD

1. What about Christ are we to reveal to the world?

   _____
   _____

2. Every one of God's children is His letter addressed to whom?

   _____
   _____

3. How can individuals who: (1) do not read the Bible, (2) do not hear God speaking to them through its pages, (3) do not see the love of God through His works, be won to love and serve Him?

   _____
   _____
   _____

4. What kind of conception of Christ and His service should people get from Christians?

   _____
   _____
   _____

5. What impressions are Christians, who gather up gloom and sadness to their souls, and murmur and complain, giving to others about God?

   _____
   _____
   _____

CHAPTER 14 - *REJOICING IN THE LORD*

6. What is the view that Satan would have us have of God?

   _____

   _____

7. How can a Christian second the falsehood of Satan? How can this be avoided?

   _____

   _____

   _____

8. How can you avoid dwelling upon your mistakes, failures and disappointments in the Christian life?

   _____

   _____

9. What are some of the pictures which God would have us contemplate or meditate on?

   _____

   _____

   _____

10. How does God feel when we by action or word reveal that we doubt His love or distrust His promises?

    _____

    _____

    _____

11. What effect does every word of doubt have upon your soul? How does this occur?

    _____

    _____

CHAPTER 14 - *REJOICING IN THE LORD*

12. What does Satan want you to do when he tempts you?

13. In addition to yourself, who can be negatively influenced by our expressions of doubt? Is it always possible to counteract your influence after you have recovered? What complicates the situation?

14. What attracts the hearts of our friends to Jesus Christ?

15. How can we brighten the life of others and strengthen their efforts?

16. Do you think it is possible to influence others, even though neither they nor you may be conscious of it? If so, explain how we can insure that our influence is for good.

17. Describe the countenance of Christ as He might have appeared to those who saw Him walk in Jerusalem. In other words, was His face happy, joyful, peaceful, or sad, gloomy, anxiety-ridden, and morose?

CHAPTER 14 - *REJOICING IN THE LORD*

18. When will you find it impossible to love others as Christ loved you? When will you find it possible to love others as Christ loves you?

19. In spite of the faults and imperfections of others which we certainly see, how should we act toward them?

20. When we talk of our difficulties, trials, anxiety, and fears what might others suppose? Is this true?

21. How can an individual today do what is stated in the following paragraph? "Some are always fearing and borrowing trouble. Everyday they are surrounded with the tokens of God's love; everyday they are enjoying the bounties of His providence; but they overlook these present blessings. Their minds are continually dwelling upon something disagreeable, which they fear may come; or some difficulty may really exist, which, though small, blinds their eyes to the many things that demand gratitude. The difficulties they encounter, instead of driving them to God, the only source of their help, separates them from Him, because they awaken unrest and repining."

CHAPTER 14 - *REJOICING IN THE LORD*

22. What will happen to us if we allow the perplexities and worries of everyday life to fret the mind and cloud the brow? What are some of the perplexities and worries of every-day life?

_____
_____
_____

23. Describe the actions we should take when threatened with loss in business?

_____
_____
_____

24. What lessons of trust did Christ seek to teach us when He referred to the birds of the air and the lilies of the field?

_____
_____
_____

25. "Happiness that is sought from selfish motives, outside of the path of duty, is ill-balanced, fitful and transitory; it passes away, and the soul is filled with loneliness and sorrow; but there is joy and satisfaction in the service of God. . . ." What point is being made by this statement?

_____
_____
_____

26. What things should we keep fresh in our memory? How do we keep these things fresh in our memory? What benefit is derived by our doing this?

_____
_____

CHAPTER 14 - *REJOICING IN THE LORD*

27. Although new perplexities and trials in the coming conflict are ahead of us, what can we depend on?

   _____

   _____

   _____

> THIS IS MY PRAYER FOR YOU, AND IT IS GOD'S PROMISE TO YOU AND ALL HIS CHILDREN.

And by and by the gates of heaven will be thrown open to admit God's children, and from the lips of the King of glory the benediction will fall on their ears like richest music.

> "COME YE BLESSED OF MY FATHER, INHERIT THE KINGDOM PREPARED FOR YOU FROM THE FOUNDATION OF THE WORLD."

Then the redeemed will be welcomed to the home Jesus is preparing for them. There their companions will not be the vile of the earth, liars, idolators, the impure, and unbelieving; but they will associate with those who have overcome Satan, and through divine grace have formed perfect characters. Every sinful tendency, every imperfection, that afflicts them here, has been removed by the blood of Christ, and the excellence and brightness of His glory, far exceeding the brightness of the sun, is imparted to them. And the moral beauty, the perfection of His character shines through them, in worth far exceeding this outward splendor. They are without fault before the great white throne, sharing the dignity and the privileges of the angels. (STEPS TO CHRIST, pp. 125,126)

APPENDIX

This appendix contains the raw answers some individuals have given as they studied these questions. Almost all answers are modified when people sit in discussion groups, in prayer meeting, in small groups. Therefore, these are not "right" answers. Right answers come as we live out—indeed take the "steps" to Christ.

STUDY WORKBOOK ANSWERS

TABLE OF CONTENTS

1.	God's Love for Man	83
2.	The Sinner's Need of Christ	88
3.	Repentance 1	91
4.	Repentance 2	94
5.	Confession	98
6.	Consecration	100
7.	Faith and Acceptance	104
8.	The Test of Discipleship	108
9.	Growing Up Into Christ	110
10.	The Walk and the Life	112
11.	A Knowledge of God	115
12.	The Privilege of Prayer	119
13.	What to Do With Doubt	124

STUDY GUIDE ANSWERS 1 - GOD'S LOVE FOR MAN

1. Nature and Revelation. (1) Nature the universe; the total of all agencies and forces in the creation. The inherent or essential qualities of anything individual constitution; sort; natural human instinct. Reality as distinct from that which is artificial. (2) Revelation. An act of revealing; that which is revealed; divine communication; the Book of Revelation.

    Nature: Creation - all of creation including man. Revelation: special revelation.

    Nature and Revelation alike testify of our Father's love.

    Nature and Revelation both speak of God's love.

    Nature. Creation: flowers, trees, birds, etc.

2. That He is someone who is tender and fatherly in His care of us, and He desires to make us happy.

    That God is love, God is someone who is kind, suffers long, seeks not His own, is not easily provoked. How-because He allows this ministry to us to continue-to comfort us.

    The message of comfort, love, and hope. God is love is written upon opening buds.

    They reveal God's love for man and bring us a message of hope and comfort, and so we know that God is love.

3. His infinite love and pity.

    God's character is love.

    God is slow to anger and, of great kindness. His infinite love and pity - His glory. The Lord, the Lord God, merciful and gracious, long-suffering and abundant in goodness and truth, keeping mercy for thousands - forgiving iniquity transgression and sin.

    That God is love, that He is merciful and gracious, long suffering and abundant in goodness and truth, keeping mercy for thousands, forgiving iniquity and transgression and sin.

    God himself has declared His infinite love and pity through His word.

    He delighteth in mercy. He is slow to anger, and of great kindness, because he delighteth in mercy.

    God's love for man.

4. Even though God is good, the devil has blinded most men and women to this fact. Instead he causes people to see God as mean and spiteful - standing on the front porch of heaven looking over the bannisters to catch us in evil.

STUDY GUIDE ANSWERS 1 - GOD'S LOVE FOR MAN

The enemy has blin ded the minds of men so that they looked upon God with fear.

Satan has blinded our eyes in many ways in regard to who God is and what He is like. In many ways we can think of God as restricting our freedom, not allowing us to do what we want - and keeping us from having fun. We think that God just wants to catch us doing wrong to punish us.

Even though God has revealed Himself in Nature, Satan has perverted Nature and man's ability to interpret Nature so much that we see God as severe and unforgiving. Also, we see Him as someone who is eager for man to sin so He can exact the full penalty of justice on man.

Many times we and others think that God is seeking to punish us for some wrong we have done. We teach this to our children and we make them afraid of God. We cause people to serve God out of fear. God is for us not against us.

Of all the wonderful, lovely things God hath given, men still see him as severe, stern.

Satan deceived men and the angels in heaven to thinking that God is an unjust God.

5. To make manifest the Father, to remove the dark shadow that Satan has placed over God's character and reveal His infinite love.

    To remove the false and untrue ideas that we have about God. To manifest the Father.

    To reveal to the world the infinite love of God. To make manifest the Father.

    To make manifest the Father. To reveal what is God like. He is the one who preaches the gospel to the poor, heals the broken hearted, delivers the captives, gives sight to the blind.

    The Lord came to heal the broken hearted, to preach deliverance to the captive, recovering of sight to the blind, to set at liberty them that are bruise.

    Jesus came to live with men to reveal to the world the infinite love of God.

6. In every act of His life.

    His compassion was revealed in every act of His life.

    Every act of His life revealed love. Even in His rebukes he revealed mercy and compassion by the tears in His voice.

    Love, mercy and compassion were revealed in every act of His life. His heart went out in tender sympathy to the children of men.

    Here on earth among men.

STUDY GUIDE ANSWERS 1 - GOD'S LOVE FOR MAN

7. This is the character of God. It is from the Father's heart that the stream of divine compassion is manifested in Christ.

   Tactful, thoughtful, kind in His attention and intercourse with people. Never rude, never speaking severe words needlessly, never giving needless pain to a sensitive soul, not censuring human weakness—always speaking the truth in love. Self denying with every soul precious in His sight. Denouncing hypocrisy, unbelief and iniquity with love.

   God of truth and love-tactful, thoughtful, never rude-sensitive to the needs of mankind—not rude. Did not condemn or blame human weakness. He understood human weakness and made provisions for it. Self denying thoughtful of others.

   The Lord God is merciful, gracious, longsuffering and abundant in goodness and truth. Slow to anger.

   Jesus exalted the truth in love with the greatest tact, thoughtful, kind attention, never rude. He did not censure human weakness.

   Merciful and gracious, longsuffering, abundant in goodness and truth, and forgiving iniquity, transgression and sin.

8. It was the burden of sin that broke the heart of God's Son; and the separation of the soul from God.

   It was the burdenof sin, the sense of its terrible enormity of its separation of the soul from God. It was this that broke the heart of the Son of God. Christ knew no sin—He had never been separated from the Father.

   Because He had been one with God. He took upon Himself the burden of sin. He who had been one with God, felt in His soul the awful separation that sin makes between God and man.

   My God, my God, why hath Thou forsaken Me? It was the burden of sin, the sense of its terrible wickedness of its separation of the soul from God.

9. Love made God act to give Jesus to the world. God already loved us, and that is why he gave us Jesus.

   God already loved the world and it was this love that caused Him to give His only begotten Son. To love us after Christ came would mean that as a result of His coming God the Father would have started loving us after Christ died. Instead He loved us FIRST and then therefore He sent Christ. His love was first.

   Love made God act—God already loved the world and therefore sent Jesus to save us. The death of Christ did not make an angry God smile or be happy. Christ was the medium through which He could pour out His infinite love upon a fallen world.

STUDY GUIDE ANSWERS 1 - GOD'S LOVE FOR MAN

God loved us already. God the Father is the source of the Gospel. Sometimes people love you because of what you do for them or because of what they have done for you. But God's love was so strong that it made Him act in our behalf.

But this great sacrifice was not made in order to create in the Father's heart a love for man, not to make Him willing to save—no, no, God so loved the world that He gave His only begotten Son. John 3:16

1. God so loved that He gave His only begotten Son. 2. Christ was the medium through which He could pour out His infinite love upon a fallen world.

Yes! God so loved the world that He gave His only begotten Son. The Father loves us not because of the great sacrifice Christ made for us, but He provided sacrifice because He loves us. God was in Christ reconciling the world unto Himself. 2 Cor. 5:19

God so loved the world that He gave His only begotten Son.

10. Christ will always be in human form.

    He is the Son of man—For all time Christ is to be in human flesh. He is our brother—One in human flesh like us.

    Christ was to identify Himself with the interest and needs of humanity. He who was one with God has linked Himself with the interest and needs of humanity. . . with ties that are never to be broken.

    None but the Son of God could accomplish our redemption. Only He who was in the bosom of the Father could declare Him; nothing less then the infinite sacrifice made by Christ could express the Father's love.

11. Because He is God, and now He is localized in space.

    Christ was the medium through which He could put out His infinite love upon the fallen world.

    Because before the incarnation Christ had filled eternity. He was one with the Father—in His bosom.

12. Exalted conceptions of what we may become through Christ.

    It should give us exalted conception of what we may become through Christ

    As sons of God, Christ elevates humanity. Through connection with Christ man may indeed become worthy of the the name sons of God.

    It should make us think of what we may become through Christ.

STUDY GUIDE ANSWERS 1 - GOD'S LOVE FOR MAN

13. We see mercy because the One on the cross is innocent. Mercy is extended to those who should hear.

    Evidence of a love that is infinite and a tender pity surpassing a mother's yearning sympathy for her wayward child.

14. We see tenderness because God has not dealt with us after our sins.

15. When we see the blood of Christ, we see the forgiveness made possible.

    Forgiveness-pardon of our sins through the blood of Jesus Christ.

    That He was willing to die for our sins, and to cleanse us from all unrighteousness.

    We see such great love that Christ had for us in our sins. He had out stretched arms of forgiveness as He hung on the cross.

16. Forgiveness.

    All are saved in the same way. He is just and yet the justifier of those who come to Him by Christ Jesus.

    God does not do away with justice at the cross nor does He do away with mercy.

17. The penalty for sin is paid—death.

    The wages of sin are paid.

    Behold what manner of love the Father has bestowed upon us that we should be called the sons of God. 1John 3:1

    He died for all.

18. When He was willing to go to Calvary for me.

    The matchless love of God for a world that did not love him. He was willing to and gave His life for them even through they couldn't even give Him their love and respect.

STUDY GUIDE ANSWERS 2 - THE SINNER'S NEED OF CHRIST

1. Well-balanced mind, noble powers, perfect in being—in harmony with God, pure thoughts, Holy aims.

2. Powers perverted, selfish, morally weak, captive to Satan—out of harmony with God.

   Perverted power, weak through transgression, he was made captive by Satan.

3. Impossible.

   Impossible in our own strength.

4. Thwart the divine plan in man's creation—to fill the earth with woe and desolation. He would say it was the result of God's work in creating man.

   It was the tempter's purpose to thwart the divine plan in man's creation, and fill the earth with woe and desolation. And he would point to all this evil as the result of God's work in creating man.

5. Because there would be no one in heaven like him—birds of a feather flock together. His thoughts, interest, motives would be alien to those that actuate the sinless dwellers there.

   The sinner could not be happy in the presence of the Holy God. Heaven to him would be a place of torture. God to them would be a consuming fire.

6. The unrenewed heart.

   The unrenewed heart it is not in harmony with God and finds no joy in communion with Him. The sinner could not be happy in God's presence.

7. They cannot change the heart, they cannot purify the springs of life. There must be a power working from above.

8. That power is Christ. His grace alone can quicken the lifeless faculties of the soul, attract it to God's holiness.

9. Heart—desires—purposes—motives—life.

10. My pursuits—the things I want in life, the things of importance are different. My reason for wanting them are different.

    The things that are sought for, change; the reasons or living, working, being; change; the things that motivate us; change. They are all new.

    In Christ we have become new creatures. We will have new Godly desire, purpose and motives in order to see the kingdom of heaven.

11. The natural person, the person not born again, does not care for spiritual things.

STUDY GUIDE ANSWERS 2 - THE SINNER'S NEED OF CHRIST

It is not enough because there is no goodness in us. Truly there is but one that is good—that is Jesus.

12. Recognize that I personally am a sinner. And that I cannot change my heart.

    Our own unspiritual condition—that we are slaves to sin.

    For we know that the law is spiritual—but I am carnal sold under sin.

    Behold I am carnal sold under sin, but I long for purity, righteousness and clean heart. My only hope is "Behold the Lamb of God which taketh away the sin of the world."

13. O wretched man that I am—who shall deliver me from this body of death—I need help.

    O wretched man that I am, who can deliver me from this body of death? I am destined to death, but I am eternally thankful that Jesus has made a way for eternal life for me.

14. Behold the Lamb of God that takes away the sin of the world.

    Behold the Lamb of God who takes away the sin of the world. This means that when I see my condition and the truth about God's holiness I need not despair, Christ will deliver me.

    Behold, the Lamb of God which taketh away the sin of the world. I am truly thankful to God, Jesus the Lamb that is there for me in spite of my sins.

15. Sadness—weighed down with a sense of guilt. Lonely, outcast, separated from all that made life dear. Fearing that his sin had cut him off from God, forsaken of heaven.

    Jacob was weighed down with guilt, lonely, separated from God, he feared his sin had cut him off from God, that He was forsaken of heaven.

16. (1) Amazing sacrifice that has been made for us. (2) The labor and energy used by heavenly agencies to reclaim the lost. (3) The exceeding rewards for right doing. (4) The enjoyment of heaven. (5) The society of angels. (6) The communion and love of God. (7) The elevation and extension of all of our powers throughout eternal ages.

    (1) The Savior's life and death and intercession, (2) the ministry of angels, (3) the pleading of the the Spirit, (4) the working of the Father, (5) the unceasing interest of heavenly beings.

17. All of the above. It takes all of these for me to make it into Heaven.

18. (1) The exceeding reward for right doing, (2) enjoyment of Heaven, (3) Angels communing with love of God and Son, (4) Elevation and extension of all our power.

19. (1) Judgment of God pronounced against sin. (2) The inevitable retribution. (3) The degradation of our character. (4) The final destruction.

STUDY GUIDE ANSWERS 2 - THE SINNER'S NEED OF CHRIST

21. Because I am a sinner—I cannot change my heart. Every day I need to die to self and live new in Christ. Every day I need to will—to choose to do God's will.

STUDY GUIDE ANSWERS 3 - REPENTANCE PART 1

1. Through Christ.

   Repent and be converted that your sins may be blotted out.

   It is only through Jesus Christ,

2. Sorrow for sin and turning away from sin.

3. To not only see the sin, sorrow, but to recognize what sin has caused over the centuries. To be reminded of the degradation of the world, man's character and to realize sin caused the death of the Son of God.

4. To turn away from it in the mind—to have no sinful desires.

   When the heart yields to influence of Holy Spirit, conscience is quickened. Holy law illuminates the secret chambers of the heart, conviction takes place.

   To repent first, then to feel what sin has caused. To allow the Lord to change your heart and give you a new one. To allow the heart to become broken so God can put it back together better.

5. They lamented the results of sin but not the sin itself.

   They lamented the suffering rather than the sin.

   The sorrow for their sin came about as a result of the problems that they had to endure. As soon as the problem went away, they returned to their sinful ways and feelings.

6. Cry, sorrow for being caught or exposed, pray, request forgiveness, pretend to lament, make an outward reformation.

   Conviction, repentance and turning away from the sin.

   We would feel sorrow primarily for the results of sin and what the consequences are instead of how bad sin really is, and how it has lowered man.

7. (1) Quickened conscience, (2) he will discern something of the depth and sacredness of God's holy law, (3) hidden things of darkness are manifested, (4) conviction takes place, (5) he sees the love of God, the beauty of holiness, the joy of purity, (6) long to be cleansed and restored to communion with heaven.

   1. The hidden things are made manifest, 2. Conviction takes hold upon the mind and heart. 3. Sense of God's righteousness. 4. Terror of God appearing. 5. Sees the love of God and beauty of holiness. 6. Long to be cleansed and restored to communion with Heaven.

8. It is dead in trespasses and sins.

STUDY GUIDE ANSWERS 3 - REPENTANCE PART 1

    Because we were dead in sins. .

9. One experiences a change from death to life, a rebirth, new life and is brought into a new relationship in which he is governed by new principles.

    Deep sorrow which leads to repentance. Then there is a desire to obey the will of God.

10. The enormity of his transgression and the defilement of his soul.

    David saw the enormity of his transgressions, defilement of his soul, and loathed his sins.

    He saw the greatness of his sin, how it defiled his soul. He hated sin. He wanted his heart to be purged.

11. Purity of heart, the joy of holiness—to be restored to harmony and communion with God. 2. His sin had erected a barrier between him and God.

12. No.

13. Jesus.

    Jesus Christ.

    Jesus Christ our Savior and Prince.

14. No. Accept Christ's invitation to come to Him and the virtue that flows from Him leads to genuine repentance.

    Come to Jesus right now.

15. When there is a desire for truth, purity and conviction of our own sinfulness.

    When there is a desire for truth, and my heart is convicted of wrong doing.

16. The goodness of God. The kindness of God is trying to lead one to make an "about-face" a change of mind, purpose and life.

    God's kindness leads to repentance; God's grace through the death of His Son and the ever present Holy Spirit are just a couple of the ways in which God leads us to repentance.

17. The incomprehensible love of Christ as manifested in His dying on the cross for sinners.

    Christ manifests a love that is incomprehensible, and as the sinner beholds His love, it softens the heart, impresses the mind, inspires the soul.

    Lamb of God on the cross of Calvary.

STUDY GUIDE ANSWERS 3 - REPENTANCE PART 1

18. In our witnessing and letting Him live out His life in us—in every word and act and in our relationship with others.

19. When they become ashamed of their sinful ways.

    When we learn to deal truly with our own souls, be as sincere, as tenacious, as you would if your life depended on it, and it does.

20. No. They have a sincere desire to change their ways but they are not always aware that it is the drawing power of Christ.

21. When we are drawn to look upon His cross to behold Him whom our sins have pierced, our heart is quickened, our wickedness is revealed to us and we begin to understand something of Christ's righteousness and our sinfulness.

    The conscience is quickened and outward life is amended.

22. He will be drawn to Jesus.

    They start to recognize the righteousness of Christ.

23. A knowledge of the plan of salvation.

24. The almighty God, creator of all things, master of nature looks upon each one of us, in our struggle of life. The Holy Spirit convicts us of sin, and leads us to a desire to repent. When we have this, the Holy Spirit helps us, guides us into the proper means of salvation.

STUDY GUIDE ANSWERS 4 - REPENTANCE PART 2

2. One ray of the glory of God, one gleam of purity of Christ, penetrating the soul, makes every spot of defilement painfully distinct, lays bare the deformity and defects of human character.

   Christ's righteousness.

   His perfect character and nature.

   The light from Christ is a true, or better, understanding of Christ, his teachings and Himself. One gleam of this purity of Christ, one ray of the glory of God. The spiritual character of the law.

3. 1. Make apparent the unhallowed desires; 2. infidelity of the heart; 3. impurity of the lips; (4) the sinner's act of disloyalty in making void the law of God.

   1. How impure we are. 2. The selfishness of motive. 3. The enmity against God that has defiled every act of life. 4. That our own righteousness is as filthy rags—and that the blood of Christ alone can cleanse us from the defilement of sin and renew our hearts in His own likeness.

4. When the soul is touched by the Holy Spirit of God, he will hate himself as he views the pure spotless character of Christ, and will seek purity of heart.

   When I see God's glory, and have a sense of my own weakness and imperfection, I will hate my selfishness of soul, and my love of myself, more than or at the expense of others, and I will want purity of heart, or a cleansing from the kind of self love and selfishness, so I can be in harmony with God and His law.

5. However trifling this or that wrong act may seem in the eyes of men, no sin is small in the sight of God.

   No. All sins are sin in sight of God. There are no small sins in God's sight.

   No sin is small in the sight of God.

6. Pride, selfishness, and covetousness, these sins are especially offensive to God. They are contrary to the benevolence of His character.

7. It (pride) closes the heart against Christ and the infinite blessings He came to give.

8. The publican was completely humble, the pharisee felt so self righteous.

   The publican felt the need of Christ in his life because he knew that he was a sinner. And he prayed to God, asking Him for mercy. The pharisee was self righteous in his prayer, and didn't feel the need of Christ.

STUDY GUIDE ANSWERS 4 - REPENTANCE PART 2

The publican not only repented and asked forgiveness for his sins; he also was deeply sorry for his sins. His prayer was a bearing of the soul. The pharisee still retained his lofty air as if forgiveness was due him from All Mighty God.

9. In Christ Jesus.

   There is help for me only through God.

   In Christ. In God.

10. We must not wait for stronger persuasions, better opportunity or holier temper. We can do nothing of ourselves. We must come to Christ as we are.

    No, because there is danger in putting off, or delaying forsaking your sins.

    No! We should acknowledge the wooing of the Holy Spirit and come to Christ just as we are.

    No. They may not come. There is danger in remaining in sin for any length of time.

11. 1. No other way in which man could be saved. 2. Without this sacrifice it was impossible for the human race to escape from the defiling power of sin. 3. Impossible to be restored to communion with holy beings. 4. Impossible for them again to become partakers of eternal life.

12. The love, suffering and death of the Son of God all testify to the terrible enormity of sin.

    By His death on the cross, through his shedding of blood. (HEB. 9:22)

    The love and suffering and death of the Son of God. By showing us that even Christ, God could not, or did not simply do away with sin, but had to suffer because of it.

13. The sins and defects of others do not excuse anyone. Those who complain of the wrong course of professed Christians should show better lives.

    The sins and defects of others is not an excuse, because we should not use another man as an example; Christ is our perfect pattern.

    The sins and defects of others do not excuse anyone, because the Lord has not given us an erring human pattern, not even the pastor, nor his wife, nor elders, nor deacons, nor other Christians.

14. If a non-Christian has so high a conception of what a Christian should be, they know what is right yet refuse to do it.

    They know to do right, but yield not to the pleading of God.

    They know what is right—which is seen in their judgment—yet they refuse to do it.

STUDY GUIDE ANSWERS 4 - REPENTANCE PART 2

15. Beware of procrastination, thousands have erred to their eternal loss. This is a terrible danger.

    1. Tomorrow is not promised. 2. Sin will overpower us without divine help. 3. Prompting of the Holy Spirit not ignored.

    Shortness and uncertainty of life. To delay is to choose to live in sin. Infinite loss is involved in delay. What we do not overcome will overcome us and work out our destruction.

16. Every act of transgression, neglect or rejection of grace of God; it is hardening the heart, depraving the will, benumbing the understanding, less capable yielding to Holy Spirit.

    1. Hardening of the heart. 2. Depraving the will. 3. Benumbing the understanding. 4. Makes you/me less inclined to yield. 5. Less capable of yielding to the tender pleading of God's Holy Spirit. Even one wrong trait of character, one sinful desire, persistently cherished, will eventually neutralize all the power of the Gospel.

17. Quieting a troubled conscience and trifling with invitations of mercy.

    The desire to change leaves the person.

    The experience and the education of a lifetime which has molded the character—shaped it's sinful habits. Every sinful indulgence strengthens the soul's aversion to God.

18. Today—if ye will hear My voice harden not your heart.

    Now! By our accepting His grace.

19. This person recognizes that only God can truly search and know their heart. This person is not willing to leave the searching of their hearts even to themselves. God only can truly search your heart.

    Asking God to examine me. My heart/motive, my character, the inner most feeling. Where there is contradictions to His will, purge me.

    This means to allow God to do exploratory spiritual surgery on me, and to remove anything that is not right with Him and I will not fight Him.

20. True religion is from the heart and soul, sincere. Intellectual religion is having knowledge of religion.

    An intellectual religion is a form of godliness, is religion without the love of God in the heart.

    Form of godliness, when heart is not cleansed. True religion deals truly with self. Earnest, sincere.

    In true religion the heart is cleansed of sin.

STUDY GUIDE ANSWERS 4 - REPENTANCE PART 2

21. Create in me a clean heart, O God, and renew a right spirit within me. Ps. 51:10

    Ask God to change your heart, and give you His spirit.

22. A new person.

    The guides weeded to see the Lord's face is peace. Convicts, convinces, show the way to eternal life. Listen!

    It convinces of sin, reveal plainly the way of salvation. It is the voice of God speaking to our souls.

23. Do not give up in despair. Christ came to save us!

    No! If it were not for my sins, Christ would never have suffered and died.

    No—because Christ came to save sinners. A person has to know that he/she/me/I/ am a sinner in order to be saved.

24. His unutterable love.

    The Holy Spirit.

    When we get to heaven, all of these questions will be answered in different degrees. Some great. Some not so great.

    God's eternal love!

25. Tell the enemy that Jesus came into the world to save sinners.

    Tell him that Christ gave His life, shed His blood so that I can receive grace, and be forgiven. "Get thee behind . . ."

    Look up to your/my Redeemer and talk of His merits. Acknowledge your sin, but tell the enemy that Christ Jesus came into the world to save sinners, and that I/you may be saved by His matchless love.

26. As we look at Calvary and come to understand it better.

    When we get to heaven, all of these questions will be answered in different degree. Some great. Some not so great.

    It is when we most fully comprehend the love of God, that we realize the sinfulness of sin, When we see how far down Christ had to reach for us, for me.

STUDY GUIDE ANSWERS 5 - CONFESSION

1. He that confesseth and forsaketh his sin shall have mercy, and He will abundantly bless us.

2. Confess faults to one another. Confess your sins to God. Sin—transgression against divine or moral law especially one that is committed consciously.

   Faults are offenses committed agamst a person. Sin is transgression of God's law. Faults are confessed to people. Sins are offenses against God. Sins are confessed to God.

3. Acknowledge your wrong to that person. Seek the forgiveness of God.

4. Because the brother you have wounded is the property of God, and in injuring him you sinned against his Creator and Redeemer.

   Because we are brothers and God's children.

5. Those who have not humbled their souls before God in acknowledging their guilt, have not yet fulfilled the first condition of acceptance. Have not experienced repentance.

6. That we are not willing to humble our hearts and comply with the conditions of the word of truth.

7. The Lord is nigh unto them that are of a broken heart. And saveth such as be of contrite spirit. Ps. 34; 18 The confession that is the outpouring of the inmost soul finds its way to the God of infinite pity.

   Because if confession is not heartfelt and freely expressed, it is not true, it is not done with the intention of forsaking it. It is not seen as being the confession of something that is really wrong.

8. They may be of such a nature as to be brought before God only. They may be wrongs that should be confessed to individuals who have suffered injury through them, or they may be of a public character, and should then be publicly confessed.

   True confession is specific—not evasive—it names the individual and particular sins that have been committed. Whether they are confession of sins or faults it should be specific.

9. In the first statement every sin that you have already confessed is already forgiven. They are forgiven at Calvary, but the forgiveness is received by us as we confess. In the second statement we have only received forgiveness for those sins that we have confessed.

   The first statement says God is ready and willing-when the truth of the matter is that when we confess it, God forgives it right then, He is ready to forgive before we confess. He forgives when we confess. The only reason we do not have remission of sins that are past is that we are not willing to humble our hearts and comply with the conditions of the word of truth. All sins confessed are forgiven. Unconfessed sins remain on the soul.

10. There must be decided changes in the life, everything offensive to God must be put away.

STUDY GUIDE ANSWERS 5 - CONFESSION

A humble and broken heart.

Repentance and reformation—decided changes in the life, everything offensive to God will be put away.

11. This kind of confession is self-justification and will not be acceptable to God. True repentance will lead a person to bear his guilt himself, and acknowledge it without deception and hypocrisy.

    When we are blinded by sin, truly we don't know what is right.

12. True repentance will lead a man to bear his guilt himself and acknowledge it without deception or hypocrisy.

13. Those who acknowledge their guilt will be justified.

    They will be justified, for Jesus will plead His blood in behalf of the repentant soul.

14. He did not seek to shield himself. He paints his sin in its darkest hue, not attempting to lessen his guilt. Jesus came into the world to save sinner of whom I am chief. 1 Tim 1:15

    Specifically. Many of the saints did I shut up in prison, having received authority from the chief priest; and when they were put to death, I have my voice against them. And I punished them oft in every synagogue, and compelled them to blaspheme, and being exceedingly mad against them, I persecuted them even unto strange cities. Acts 26: 10,11. He said that Christ Jesus came into the world to save sinners; of whom I am chief

15. The humble and broken heart, subdued by genuine repentance, will appreciate something of the love of God and the cost Calvary.

STUDY GUIDE ANSWERS 6 - CONSECRATION

1. The act of consecrating (to set apart as sacred or holy). The condition of being consecrated. To devote to a purpose.

2. To give oneself completely and without reservation. It is necessary or the change can never be wrought in us by which we are to restored to His likeness.

   The whole heart must be yielded to God, or the change can never be wrought in us by which we are to be restored to His likeness. This requires an entire transformation, renewing of our whole nature.

   Total commitment. Death to self. Our whole being; by nature we are alienated from God. The Holy Spirit describes our condition is being dead in trespasses and sin.

3. We are restored to His likeness.

   He will heal us and set us free, a renewing of our whole nature.

   The whole heart must be yielded to God and must yield ourselves wholly to Him, and there will be an entire transformation, a renewing of our whole nature.

4. The warfare against self is the greatest battle that was ever fought. The yielding of self, surrendering all to the will of God, requires a struggle, but the soul must submit to God before it can be renewed in holiness.

5. It appeals to the intellect, mind or conscience.

   The yielding of self, surrendering all to the will of God, requires a struggle, but the soul must submit to God before it can be renewed in holiness. You can choose to serve him, give him your will.

   It requires a struggle, it appeals to the intellect and conscience. God does not force us, He invites us to come let us reason together. He invites us to give ourselves, that He may work His will in us.

6. An unreasoning control.

   To force the will of His creatures.

7. A person or animal who's actions are merely mechanical without thought like a machine.

8. A mere forced submission would prevent all real development of mind or character.

   Would prevent all real development of mind or character. It would make a man a mere automaton.

STUDY GUIDE ANSWERS 6 - CONSECRATION

It would prevent all real development of mind or character. He has something better to offer to us, than what we are seeking for ourselves.

9. Come let us reason together.

   He invites us to give ourselves to Him, that He may work His will in us. It remains for us to choose whether we will be set free from the bondage of sin, to share the glorious liberty of the sons of God.

   He appeals to the intellect and the conscience. God desires that man, the crowning mark of His creative power, shall reach the highest possible development.

10. We must repent and ask God to forgive us of our sins.

    In giving ourselves to God, we must necessarily give up ail that would separate us from Him.

    We must be willing to come to God, letting Christ Jesus come into our hearts.

11. Money, gold, silver.

    Money, reputation, desire of wealth, wealth, worldly honor.

    Mammon is the idol of many. The love of money, the desire for wealth, is the golden chain that binds them to Satan.

    The love of money, worldly honor, the life of selfish ease, and freedom from responsibility.

12. Those who profess to serve God, while they rely upon their own efforts to obey His law, to form a right character and secure salvation. Their hearts are not moved by any deep sense of the love of Christ.

13. Christ will be the spring of action in them.

    Those who feel the constraining love of God do not ask how little may be given to meet the requirements of God, they do not ask for the lowest standard, but aim at perfect conformity to the will of their Redeemer.

14. We should ask God to give us a change of heart.

    Ask yourself the question "What has Christ given for me?" The Son of God gave all—life and love and suffering for our redemption. We should not withhold our hearts from Him.

15. He purifies and cleanses by His own blood and saves by His matchless love.

16. When we think and act contrary to the will of God.

STUDY GUIDE ANSWERS 6 - CONSECRATION

17. To me it means God has a plan to give me—I truly obey and follow Him.

    When we know God's Word is true and we decide to "do it our way," then we find ourselves in trouble for being disobedient to the will of God.

    God knows what is best for us and plans good for us.

18. No. God does not want His children to suffer.

    No. John 3:16. All heaven is interested in the happiness of man. Our heavenly Father does not close the avenues of joy to any of His creatures.

19. Peace and joy.

    It is His purpose to impart peace and rest to all who come to Him for the bread of life.

    His love and character.

20. Use the power of choice to choose Christ.

    Consent to wear His yoke, to bear His burden, choose to serve Him.

    Knowing that we can do nothing of ourselves to save, we have to yield all to the will of God.

21. That is, depend on the right exercise of the will.

    This is the governing power in the nature of man, the power of decision, or of choice. Everything depends on the right action of the will.

22. Governing power is that which controls—governs. He will then work in you to will and to do according to His good pleasure. Thus your whole nature will be brought under the control of the Spirit of Christ.

    He will work in you, and give you His Spirit.

23. Yes it is.

    Many will be lost while hoping and desiring to be Christians. They do not come to the point of yielding the will to God. They do not choose to be Christians.

    Yes. If we do not come to the point of yielding the will to God, our desire for goodness and holiness means very little.

24. By turning my will into God's will.

STUDY GUIDE ANSWERS 6 - CONSECRATION

Through the right exercise of the will an entire change may be made in your life. By yielding up your will to Christ.

STUDY GUIDE ANSWERS 7 - FAITH AND ACCEPTANCE

1. Of sin, of righteousness, of judgment, will see your faults.

2. Your motives are impure your heart is unclean, you see that your life has been filled with selfishness and sin. You long to be forgiven, to be cleansed, to be set free.

   That I am unclean, and the life is filled with selfishness and sin.

3. We must ask Jesus. Believe and reach out to Him for help.

   It is peace that you need—Heaven's forgiveness, peace and love in the soul. Money cannot buy it. You can never hope by your own efforts to secure it. But God offers it to you as a gift, without money and without price. Isaiah 55:1.

   Only by God through Jesus Christ.

4. A person reasons with God through a reading of the Bible. The Bible is a discerner of the thoughts and intents of the heart. God says compare what you think to My Word. Prayerfully think things through—look at life—what, why, when, where, who, how—what has happened, what was right, what was wrong. Look at what happened as opposed to what was promised, expected. Discern the places God spoke to you.

5. No matter how bad my sins have been, God can remove them and the residue of them. He promises to do this.

   Even before we have recognized the fact that we are sinners, Christ promises complete cleansing and purification.

   That means we come and talk with God. He knows all about us.

   He will make the red crimson, pure and white as wool if we sincerely confess our sins. The Lord will forgive us and give us a new heart and a new spirit will be put within us. Ezekiel 36:26.

   He will make you brand new. Make our sins that are deep stained, pure and clean.

6. 1. Confessed my sins. 2. Repentance—in heart put them away. 3. Consecration—Resolved to give myself to Him.

   We must believe that Jesus will give us a new heart. He promised that He would.

   You cannot atone for your past sins. You cannot change your heart and make yourself holy. 1. You believe that promise, 2. you confess your sins, 3. and give yourself to God.

7. Because He said, though your sin be like scarlet He will make us white as snow, and the Lord keeps His promises.

STUDY GUIDE ANSWERS 7 - FAITH AND ACCEPTANCE

If you believe the promised, believe that you are forgiven and cleansed. God supplies the fact, you are made whole just as Christ gave the paralytic power to walk. It is so if you believe it.

Because He has promised it, I believe it.

8. A new heart also will I give you, and a new spirit will I put within you; and I will take away the stony heart out of your flesh, and I will give you an heart of flesh. And I will put my spirit within you, and cause you to walk in my statutes, and ye shall keep my judgments and do them. Ezekiei 36; 26, 27

9. We must believe we do receive and it is ours.

   We must have faith in Him. Believe His promise. He keeps His word.

10. To inspire them with confidence in Him concerning things which they could not see. Leading them to believe in His power to forgive sins.

11. He willed to walk and he did walk.

    The man believed the words of Jesus. There was power in Jesus' word. Also the man acted on the word of God.

    Rise, take up thy bed, and walk. He believed Christ's word. Believed that he was made whole, and he made the effort at once, he willed to walk and he did walk.

12. He acted on the word of Christ, and God gave the power. He was made whole.

13. I cannot atone for my past sins, I cannot change my heart or make myself holy. But God promises to atone for my past sins, and to change my heart and to make me holy. I believe Him.

    In like manner you are a sinner. You cannot atone for your past sins, you cannot change your heart and make yourself holy. But God promised to do all this for you.

14. (1) Confess my sins, (2) give myself to God, (3) will—choose to serve Him. I choose to serve Him.

    (1) Believe that promise, (2) confess your sins, and (3) give yourself to God. God will fulfill His word to you. Will to serve.

15. I must trust God's promise that He has cleansed me from my sin.

    Do not wait to feel that you are made whole but say I believe it, it is so, not because I feel it but because God has promised.

    Believe it because God has promised, believe that you have been forgiven.

STUDY GUIDE ANSWERS 7 - FAITH AND ACCEPTANCE

Yes it is God's will that we live clean and righteous lives.

17. Thank God for the blessing that He gives.

    Give thanks that we have received.

18. If you are in Christ you have no condemnation.

19. This statement means that God through Jesus Christ paid something—paid someone for me. Because I am not a thing, God did not pay things for me. He paid for me with Someone—His own Precious Jesus Christ. Christ paid for me with His life. Christ is the best of the best of the best. . . .

    The price paid for my redemption is beyond my ability to pay or even to calculate. You were not redeemed with things that perish away. For Christ to have blood, He had to become a man, this is an inestimable sacrifice. As a Lamb without blemish and without spot, He had to be a sinless man who had blood, to die, to atone for my sin. Praise God! Hallelujah.

    That I was purchased by the precious blood of Christ.

20. Do not draw back. Say I am Christ's, I have given myself to Him.

    Thank you God for the new life which I have in your Son

    I am Christ's, I have given myself to Him and ask Him to give me His Spirit and keep me by His grace. As it is by giving yourself to God, and believing Him, that you become His child, so you are to live in Him.

21. Ask Him to give you His Spirit and keep you by His grace.

    To cleanse me from sin and try by God's grace to live a Holy life.

22. You are to remain in Christ by constantly doing the same thing that brought you to Christ.

    In the same way that I received Him: understanding God's love for man; knowing my need for Christ; repentance, confession; consecration; having faith in God and accepting Him every day.

    Walk ye in Him. Taking the same steps day by day.

23. We can claim the blessing right now.

    Now! just as we are.

24. I (you) can come to Christ just as I am.

STUDY GUIDE ANSWERS 7 - FAITH AND ACCEPTANCE

Christ bids us come to Him just as we are, weak, foolish, sinful, and when we fail at His feet, acknowledging Him as righteous, and repenting of our sins. He closes us in His arms, so that others cannot really see how weak, foolish, and sinful we are. And then He heals us. He cleanses us.

25. Me and you.

    Every repentant transgressor.

    To all who accept. . . . they are the expression of unutterable love and pity. The great heart of Infinite Love is drawn toward the sinner with boundless compassion. "We have redemption through His blood, the forgiveness of sin." Ephesians 1:7. Yes, only believe that God is your helper. He wants to restore His moral image in man. As you draw near to Him with confession and repentance, He will draw near to you with mercy and forgiveness.

    All who He has made (man) and will accept Him.

26. Jesus died that I might live. He loves me and wills not that I should perish. I have a compassionate Heavenly Father and although I have abused His love, though the blessings He has given me have been squandered, I will arise and go to my Father, and say, I have sinned against heaven, and before Thee, and am no more worthy to be called Thy son, make me as one of Thy hired servants.

    We should say, Jesus has died that I might live. He loves me.

27. To entertain the thought that when a sinner—you, me, any person—wants to come to God, when we long to return to Him, the Lord sternly withholds us from coming to His feet in repentance.

    Believing that God hinders sinners, who long to return to Him, longs to forsake sinners from coming to His feet in repentance.

28. He will draw near to you with mercy and forgiveness.

STUDY GUIDE ANSWERS 8 - A TEST OF DISCIPLESHIP

7. No. Someone could fake it, even speaking in tongues, even then the devil is powerful, and it can be him that causes people to fake this. Speaking in tongues can be a learned behavior.

   No, we cannot trust that at all.

8. Those who become new creatures in Christ Jesus will bring forth the fruits of the Spirit, love, joy, peace, long suffering, gentleness, goodness, faith, meekness, temperance. A change will be seen in the character, the habits, the pursuits.

9. Our thoughts are of Him, we long to bear His image, breathe His spirit, do His will, and please Him in all things.

   Our sweetest thoughts are of Him. He has our heart, our thoughts, our conversation, our warmest affections, our best energies.

10. Ourselves, or our good works, for we can do nothing to change the heart or bring ourselves into harmony with God.

    We must not trust ourselves or our good works. Our lives will reveal whether the grace of God is dwelling within us.

11. Character, habits, pursuits.

    If the heart has been revealed by the Spirit of God, the life will bear witness.

12. There is no evidence of genuine repentance unless it works reformation. There is a change in the life. He gives back that he has robbed, confesses his sins, and loves God and his fellow man.

    No. Repentance is turning the mind and the life around.

13. Duty becomes a delight, and sacrifice a pleasure when we come to Christ and become partakers of His pardoning grace. Love springs up in the heart, burdens are lighter, the yoke is easy.

14. 1.Looking to their own works, trusting to anything they can do, to bring themselves into harmony with God.

    2.Believes in Christ releases us from keeping the law of God. That works have nothing to with our redemption.

15. Obedience, the service and allegiance of love. This is the love of God that we keep his commandments. Here is the true test: If we abide in Christ, if the love of God dwells in us, our feelings, our thoughts, our purpose, our actions will be in harmony with the will of God as expressed in the precepts of His holy law.

16. Love of Christ. In the heart renewed by divine grace, love is the principle of action. It modifies character, governs the impulses, controls the passions, subdues enmity, ennobles the affections.

STUDY GUIDE ANSWERS 8 - A TEST OF DISCIPLESHIP

17. The more faulty we appear in our own eyes. A view of our sinfulness drives us to Him, who can pardon our sins and will reveal Himself in power.

18. No. A person may not be able to tell the exact time or place or trace all the chain of circumstances in the process of conversion.

    No. We can not always tell the time or place, but when we have been truly born our lives will show it.

19. No. By grace are ye saved through faith, but faith if it hath not works is dead.

    No works that we do will every get us into heaven, because we are saved by grace.

    We do not earn salvation by our obedience, for salvation is the free gift of God, to be received by faith. Because of the fall of Adam our natures are sinful and unholy, and all our righteous acts are tainted.

STUDY GUIDE ANSWERS 9 - GROWING UP INTO CHRIST

1. If we are not born again, we cannot have a Spiritual life or abide in Christ.

2. No growth is produced in plants by care, anxiety, and effort. It is only through the life of which God Himself has implanted that either plant or animal can live.

3. Water, air, sunshine, and nutrients in the soil.

4. The plants and flowers grow not by their own care or anxiety or effort, but by receiving that which God has furnished. No more can you of yourself secure spiritual growth.

5. All who choose to breathe this life giving atmosphere will live and grow up to the stature of men and women in Christ Jesus.

6. We are dependent upon Christ. We must remain in a relationship with Him in order to grow.

7. Our union with Christ. It is by communion with Him daily, hourly, by abiding in Him that we grow in grace.

8. We are to give ourselves to Christ. Our hearts, our wills, our service—give ourselves to Him to obey all His requirements.

9. Take My yoke upon you and ye shall find rest. Take His yoke—His interest—His work.

10. In the morning when I first wake, thank God for the day, ask Him to be with me, and ask Him to take care of me. Make me wholly Thine.

11. Take me O Lord, and make me as wholly Thine. On Christ.

12. Consecrate yourself to God each morning, let Him be first, ask Him to be with us this day every step of the way.

13. Let your mind dwell upon His love, upon the beauty, the perfection, of His character. Christ in His self-denial, Christ in His humiliation, Christ in His purity, and holiness, Christ in His matchless love.

14. By loving Him, copying Him, depending wholly upon Him, that you are to be transformed into his likeness.

15. Abide in me—the idea of rest, of stability, confidence in Him. Rest in labor, rest while working.

16. (1) Pleasures of the world, (2) life's cares and perplexities and sorrows, (3) the faults of others, or (4) your own faults and imperfections.

17. It turns the soul away from Christ, the source of our strength.

STUDY GUIDE ANSWERS 9 - GROWING UP INTO CHRIST

18. "I live; yet not I, but Christ liveth in me: and the life which I now live in the flesh I live by faith. . . ." Galations 2:20

19. By choosing to separate ourselves from Christ.

20. We are always free to do this. But let us keep our eyes fixed on Christ.

21. I think these statements are true, because God gives us this power to choose to stay with Him or to follow Satan. We have to choose.

22. We are to behold Christ in life—in His Word—in nature. Beholding Christ we are changed into the same image, from glory to glory even as by the Spirit of the Lord.

23. John did not really possess that loveliness of character. He was not only self-assertive and ambitious for honor, but impetuous, and resentful under injuries.

24. Humbled, patience, tenderness, meekness.

25. The power of love of Christ wrought a transformation in John's heart.

26. Their union with Him was closer then when He was personally with them. The light, and love, and power of the indwelling Christ shone out through them, so that men, beholding, marveled, and they took knowledge of them.

27. They knew that Jesus would be with them always.

28. His Holy Spirit.

29. Receive all He gives. Rest in laboring with Christ. Choose to remain with Him, and in Him. Think, meditate, talk much of Christ.

STUDY GUIDE ANSWERS 10 - THE WORK AND THE LIFE

1. Blessings-life of God.

    Like rays of light from the sun, like the streams of water bursting from a living spring. It is the life of God.

    The life of God. When God's life is in the heart it will flow out.

2. Working for happiness of others, the uplifting and redemption of fallen men.

3. Ministering to those who are wretched and in every way inferior in character and rank.

4. 1. The spirit of Christ's self-sacrificing love is the spirit that pervades heaven and is the very essence of its bliss.

    2. Ministering to those who are wretched and in every way inferior in character and rank, is thought of as humiliating.

5. In a desire to work as He worked for the blessing and uplifting of humanity. Leading to love, tenderness and sympathy toward all the creatures of our heavenly Father.

6. For the salvation of lost mankind.

    He worked for the blessing and uplifting of humanity, for the salvation of lost mankind.

7. Yes.

    Every day of His life Christ willingly followed one path that caused Him to deny His own will, Christ did not have it easy here. He endured want, privation, hunger, doing without, disappointment. But His own needs He denied, and made them serve His one purpose of saving man.

8. Make any sacrifice, that others for whom He died may share the heavenly gift.

9. A desire to make known to others what a precious Friend they have found in Christ.

10. Behold the Lamb of God which taketh away the sins of the world. Attractions to world to come.

    That Christ is our only hope to escape the troubles of this world and to give us peace in the world to come.

    There will be an intensity of desire to follow in the path that Jesus trod and a longing that those around us may behold the Lamb of God which taketh away the sins of the world.

    What attracted me to Christ: His acceptance, the enrichment of my mind. The joy of seeing Him, and the sinless angels and beings from other worlds.

STUDY GUIDE ANSWERS 10 - THE WORK AND THE LIFE

11. Those who become participants in labors of love are brought nearest to their Creator. Through my ministry.

    The effort to bless others will react in blessings upon ourselves. When we help others it always turns out as a blessing to ourselves.

12. He has granted men the privilege of becoming partakers of the divine nature and in their turn, of diffusing blessings to their fellow man.

13. Those who thus become participants in labor of love are brought nearest to their Creator.

14. Because He (God) loves us, He chooses to make us co-workers with Christ and the angels, that we might share the blessings, the joy, the spiritual uplifting, which results from this unselfish ministry.

15. Every act for the good of others strengthens the spirit of beneficence in the giver's heart, allying him more closely to the Redeemer of this world.

    It brings us closer to Him, therefore, we can see how much He loves us, that He would bear the suffering that we are suppose to dear.

    We begin to feel with Christ the terrible results of sin in our own being, and the terrible cost of sin, especially when we see how difficult it is to break its chains in our lives and the lives of others, therefore, we agonize with God for deliverance.

16. Drive you to the Bible and prayer. You will grow in grace and the knowledge of Christ, and develop a rich experience.

17. It will give you depth, stability, and Christlike loveliness to the character, and brings peace and happiness to its possessor.

    The spirit of unselfish labor for others gives depth, stability and Christlike loveliness to the character, and brings peace and happiness to its possessor.

18. Be disinterestedly doing the very work which Christ has enjoined upon us, engaging to the extent of our ability, in helping and blessing those who need the help we can give them.

19. We have to exercise our God given power to grow up in Christ.

    Strength comes by exercise, activity is the very condition of life. The Christian who will not exercise his God-given powers, not only fails to grow up in Christ, but he loses the strength that he already had.

    Use it—exercise it—or lose it. Eating good food, doing no exercise will make you fat, lazy, and complaining.

STUDY GUIDE ANSWERS 10 - THE WORK AND THE LIFE

20. He not only fails to grow up into Christ, but he loses the strength that he already had.

21. With our means (money), our sympathy, and our prayers.

    Prayers, finances, encouragement to others to go.

22. In the home circle, in the church, among those with whom we associate, and with whom we do business.

    In our home circle, or where ever duty lies.

23. In His workshop at His humble trade as a carpenter. In the humblest duties and lowliest positions of life, we may walk with, and work with Christ.

    So that we may know that in the humblest duties and lowliest positions of life, we may walk and work with Jesus. At His humble trade walking beside peasants and laborers, unrecognized, unhonored.

24. Because others were possessed of superior endowments and advantages, and form the opinion that only those who are especially talented are required to consecrate their abilities to the service of God.

25. We are fitting ourselves for the higher work and the unshadowed joy of the life to come.

STUDY GUIDE ANSWERS 11 - A KNOWLEDGE OF GOD

1. 1. Green fields. 2. Lofty trees. 3. Buds and flowers. 4. Passing clouds. 5. Falling rain. 6. Babbling brooks.

2. That His lessons might thus be often recalled to mind even amid the busy cares of man's life of toil.

3. The beauty of character, purity and simplicity.

   God loves beauty of character.

4. He would have us cultivate purity and simplicity.

   If we would listen, God's created work will teach us precious lessons of obedience and trust.

5. To obey the Creator's will.

   The stars in their course through space, follow from age to age their appointed path down to the minutest atom the things of nature, obey the Creator's will.

6. Everything that He created, He upholds the unnumbered worlds, cares for the little sparrows.

   God cares for everything, and sustains everything that He created. By upholding the unnumbered worlds throughout infinite space. That we know He cares for us.

   God cares for everything and sustains everything that He has created.

7. No tears are shed that God does not notice. There is no smile that He does not mark.

   That God is always there for us, each one of us is tenderly watched by the heavenly Father.

   If we would but fully believe this, all undue anxieties would be dismissed. Our lives would not be so filled with disappointment as now. We should then enjoy a rest of soul to which many have long been strangers.

8. Think of the world that is to come.

   We should think of the world that is to come. The home of the saved, and remember the promise, that it will be more glorious than we can ever imagine. In all the beautiful gifts of God in nature we can see but the faintest gleaming of His glory. "It is written, Eye hath not seen, nor ear heard, neither have entered into the heart of man, the things which God hath prepared for them that love Him." 1 Cor. 2:9.

   Think of the world that is to come that shall never know the blight of sin and death; where the face of nature will no more wear the shadow of the curse.

9. He recognizes his Father's handiwork and perceives His love in flowers, shrubs and trees.

STUDY GUIDE ANSWERS 11 - A KNOWNLEDGE OF GOD

Because the Christian recognizes his Father's handiwork, and looks on them as an expression of God's love for man.

10. Circumstances and surroundings, changes daily taking place around us. The way things workout in our life.

    Our circumstances and surroundings, in the changes that are daily taking place around us. By keeping the heart open to discern the goodness of God, "Who is wise, and will observe these things, even they shall understand the loving-kindness of the Lord." Ps. 33:5, 107:43.

11. David fasted and prayed all night, but God's will was done. David must have understood the workings of God, and did comfort himself after the death of the child.

    But now he is dead, wherefore should I fast, can I bring him back again. I shall go to him, but he shall not return to me.

    David fasted and prayed while the child was alive, but when the child dies he rose up and washed and went to worship. When asked about it, He said who can tell whether God will be gracious to me, that the child may live: Now he is dead wherefore should I fast.

12. God speaks to us in His work. Here we have in clearer lines (1) the revelation of His character, (2) His dealings with men, and (3) the great work of redemption.

13. They were men subject to like passion as we are. James 5:17. Example of how they struggled through discouragements like our own. How they fell under temptation as we have done, yet took heart again, and conquered by God's grace.

12. Christ.

    In John 5:39, Jesus said, "Search the scriptures for in them ye think ye have eternal life and they are they which testify of Me."

15. By reading, studying, and meditating on the Word of God.

    By studying the word of God we fill the whole heart with thoughts of God and Christ. By beholding Christ, we are changed to be like Him.

16. The words that I (Jesus) speak unto you they are spirit and they are life. John 6:53,63. Our bodies are built up from what we eat and drink and as in the natural economy, so in the Spiritual economy. It is what we meditate upon that will give tone and strength to our spiritual nature.

17. The theme of redemption is one that the angels desire to look into, it will be the science and the song of the redeemed throughout the ceaseless ages of eternity.

STUDY GUIDE ANSWERS 11 - A KNOWLEDGE OF GOD

18. 1. Our faith and love will grow stronger. 2. Our prayers will be more and more acceptable to God because they will be mixed with faith and love. 3. We will have a daily living experience in His power to save to the uttermost all that come to God.

19. We will desire to be wholly transformed and renewed in the image of His purity, and become like Him in all things.

    We shall desire to be wholly transformed and renewed in the image of His purity. A hungering and thirsting of soul to become like Him.

20. The more our thoughts are upon Christ, (2) the more we shall speak of Him to others and (2) represent Him to the world.

21. None will mistake and lose their way except those who follow their own judgment instead of the plainly revealed will of God.

22. We should study the Bible for ourselves, and not take the testimony of any man.

    We should study God's word for ourselves, and when we are told something we should search the Scriptures for ourselves to see if it is true. We can only grow in grace and a true knowledge of God by feasting on His Word. We should compare scripture with scripture and spiritual things with spiritual.

23. (1.) Men would have a breath of mind, (2) a nobility of character, and (3) a stability of purpose rarely seen in these times.

    A knowledge of God through His Word will give (1) a breath of mind, (2) a nobility of character, and (3) a stability of purpose rarely seen in these times.

24. 1. It's relation to the plan of salvation. 2. How you live it out in your life.

    (1.) One passage studied until its significances is clear to the mind, and (2) its relationship to the plan of salvation is evident. John 5:39.

25. At work, waiting in a office, even while you are walking the street.

    When you have the opportunity, even while you are walking along the pathways or the streets.

    Even while your are walking the streets you may read a passage and meditate upon it, thus fixing it in the mind.

26. We should ask for the enlightenment of the Holy Spirit, and it will be given thee. We should seek Him for light, to know what is truth.

    Never should the Bible be studied without prayer before opening its pages. We should ask for the enlightenment of the Holy Spirit, and it will be given.

STUDY GUIDE ANSWERS 11 - A KNOWNLEDGE OF GOD

27. The Holy Spirit exalts and glorifies the Savior.

    The Holy Spirit teaches us the divine truth, and leads us to do the right thing.

28. It is His office to present Christ, the purity of His righteousness and the great salvation that we have through Him. God gave His Son to die for us; and appoints His Spirit to be man's teacher and continual guide. The Holy Spirit exalts, and glorifies the Savior.

STUDY GUIDE ANSWERS 12 - THE PRIVILEGE OF PRAYER

1. He (Christ) taught us to present our daily needs before God.

   In order to commune with God, we must say to Him something concerning our actual life.

3. To present (1) their daily needs before God, and (2) to cast all their cares upon Him.

4. Our Savior identified Himself with <u>our</u> needs and weaknesses, in that He became a supplicant, a petitioner, seeking from His Father fresh supplies of strength, that He might come forth braced for duty and trial.

   His humanity, he endured struggles and tortures of soul in a world of sin.

   Jesus was often in prayer seeking from His Father fresh supplies of strength that he might come forth braced for duty and trials. He found it a comfort and joy in communion with His Father.

5. Our heavenly Father awaits to bestow upon us the fullness of His blessing.

6. On opening our hearts to God in prayer, God knows when the heart is open to the Spirit's influence, so God's blessing can be received.

6. The darkness of the evil one encloses those who neglect to pray. The whispered temptations of the enemy entice them to sin and it is all because they do not make use of the privileges that God has given them in the divine appointment of prayer.

   A. You will lose the way to the path of right doing, and the soul can not flourish when prayer is neglected, by not keeping open the communion between Jesus and your own soul. B. Go where prayer is wont to be made, pray any place and any where.

8. 1. Our need of help from Him, He has promised: I will pour water upon him that is thirsty, and floods upon the dry ground. Isaiah 44:3. 2. Faith. Those who hunger and thirst after righteousness who long after God, may be sure that they will be filled. 3. Ask and it shall be given you. 4. Prayer and perseverance.

   1. Our need of help from him. 2. Faith. 3. Forgive others (who sin against us). 4. Diligence in prayer (perseverance).

   1. We feel our need of help from him, He has promised: I will pour water upon him that is thirsty. 2. We must pray always if we would grow in faith and experience. 3. We are to be instant in prayer. 4. Watch in the same way with thanksgiving.

9. If we cling to any known sin, the Lord will not hear us, But the prayer of the penitent contrite soul is always accepted when all wrongs are righted.

   We must make right all known wrongs.

STUDY GUIDE ANSWERS 12 - THE PRIVILEGE OF PRAYER

10. He that cometh to God must believe that He is, and that He is a rewarder of them that diligently seek Him. Hebrews 11:6. When ye pray believe that ye receive them, and ye shall have them.

    What things so ever ye desire, when you pray, <u>believe</u> that you receive them, and ye shall have them Mark 11:24.

    To trust God and take Him at His word.

11. We are shortsighted, all we ask for is not always best for us.

    Because we are erring in our ways, and shortsighted that we sometimes ask for things that would not be a blessing to us.

12. Continue to pray.

    Cling to the promise, for the time of answering will surely come, and we shall receive the blessings we need most.

    We are still to believe that the Lord will answer our prayers, according to His will, that will be the best for us. We are to cling to the promises of God.

13. Perplexities will only increase and deepen.

14. As we really are.

    We are to come to God feeling helpless and dependent, as we really are in humble trusting faith.

    Feeling helpless and dependent, humble, trusting in faith, make known our wants to Him whose knowledge is infinite, who sees everything in creation, and who governs everything by His will and word.

15. If we expect our own prayers to be heard, we must forgive others in the same manner and to the same extent as we hope to be forgiven.

    Forgive us our debts as we forgive our debtors. We are to be willing to forgive others.

16. We are to be willing to forgive others as often and as much as Christ forgives us, no matter how often we are wronged.

17. We are to be instant in prayer, to continue in prayer, and watch with thanksgiving. Because the Lord Jesus is our example.

    We must pray always and stay in communion with God.

18. They will be seen in the prayer meeting.

STUDY GUIDE ANSWERS 12 - THE PRIVILEGE OF PRAYER

In prayer meeting, faithful to do their duty and earnest and anxious to reap all the benefits they can gain.

19. 1. Family circle. 2. Public prayer. 3. Secret prayer.

20. Secret prayer - this is the life of the soul.

    Secret prayer, our secret closet.

21. Prayerful state of mind. God is our tower of strength.

    Your heart be often uplifted to God. Silent prayers rise like precious incense before God.

    When our mind is stayed on God—lifting up our hearts in the spirit of earnest prayer.

22. There is no time or place which is inappropriate to offer up a petition to God.

24. Keep your wants, your joys, your sorrows, your cares, your fears before God. You cannot burden Him.

23. There is nothing in our lives too dark, or difficult that we cannot pray about to God.

    There is no chapter in our experience too dark for Him to read, there is no perplexity too difficult for Him to unravel.

25. Pray in the mind and spirit of Jesus.

    Whatever you ask of God the Father in Jesus' name and I will pray the Father for you. It is to pray in the mind and spirit of Jesus.

    It is to pray in the mind and spirit of Jesus while we believe His promises, rely upon His grace, and work His works.

26. Their prayers will become a formal routine.

27. They lose the subject matter of prayer and have no incentive to devotion. Their prayers become personal and selfish. They cannot pray in regard to the wants of humanity or the upbuilding of Christ's kingdom, pleading for strength where with to work.

28. The truth of His word lose their vividness and importance in our minds. Our hearts ceased to be enlightened and aroused by their sanctifying influence and we decline in spirituality.

    When men take themselves out of social life, away from the spheres of Christian duty and cross bearing; when they cease to work earnestly for the Master who worked earnestly for them, they lose the subject matter of prayer and have no incentive to devotion.

STUDY GUIDE ANSWERS 12 - THE PRIVILEGE OF PRAYER

We sustain a loss when we neglect the privilege of associating together to strengthen and encourage one another in the service of God.

29. It brings us into sympathy with others and is a means of development and strength to us in the service of God.

30. Christians associating together, speaking to each other about of the love of God, and the precious truths of redemption.

    This will brings us into sympathy with others.

31. If Christians would associate together, speaking to each other of the love of God and of precious truths of redemption, their own hearts would be refreshed and they would refresh one another. We should talk about what He's done for us.

    We should think and talk more of Jesus and less of self

32. Because we have an interest in them. Our friends because we love them. Our joys and our sorrows are bound with them.

33. Because we love them, we have infinitely greater reason to love God. Because its a joy to talk of His goodness, and tell of His power.

34. Giving thanks, of God's mercies, gratitude. Praise Him for what He has done for us.

    Our devotional exercises should not consist wholly in asking and receiving, but in thanksgiving to God.

35. That which is done for the glory of God should be done with cheerfulness with songs of praise and thanksgivings not with sadness and gloom. .

36. Christ and Him crucified.

    Think of the Cross, Christ, and Him crucified.

37. We should keep In our thoughts every blessing we receive from God. When we realize His great love, we should be willing to trust everything to the hand that was nailed to the cross for us.

    In our thoughts and hearts by trusting every thing to the hands of God.

38. God is worshipped in the courts above with song, music, and praise. Let us with reverent joy come before our Creator with thanksgiving and the voice of melody. Isaiah 51:3.

STUDY GUIDE ANSWERS 12 - THE PRIVILEGE OF PRAYER

God is worshipped with songs and music in the courts above, and as we express our gratitude, we are approximating to the worship of the Heavenly host. Whoso offer praise glorifieth God. Psalms 50:23. Let us with reverent joy come before our Creator with thanksgiving and the voice of melody. Isaiah 51:3.

STUDY GUIDE ANSWERS 13 - WHAT TO DO WITH DOUBT

1. Many especially those who are young in the Christian life are at times troubled with suggestions of skepticism.

   In the Bible are many things which they cannot explain, or even understand. How shall I know the right way? If the Bible indeed is the word of God, how can I be freed from doubts and perplexities?

   Those who are young in the Christian life are sometimes troubled with doubt or disbelief.

2. There are many things in the Bible which they cannot explain or even understand, and Satan employs these to shake their faith in the scripture as a revelation from God.

3. Our reason, and this testimony is abundant.

4. To the keenest intellect, the most highly educated mind, that Holy Being must ever remain clothed in mystery, we have limited understanding.

   The minds that have definable limits, the mind of man, canst thou by searching find out God? Canst thou find out the Almighty unto perfection? It is as high as heaven, what canst thou do? deeper than hell; what canst thou know? Job 11:7, 8.

6. We may discern boundless love and mercy united to infinite power. We can understand as much of His purpose as it is for own good to know.

   His boundless love and mercy united to infinite power. We can understand as much of His purposes as it is for our good to know; and beyond this we must still trust the hand that is omnipotent, the heart that's full of love.

7. We can so far comprehend His dealing with us, and the motive by which He is actuated, that we may discern boundless love and mercy united to infinite power. For then we can understand much of His purpose as it is for our good to know.

   We must still trust the hand that is omnipotent, the heart that is full of love.

   Trust God who knows the end from the beginning, and does what is best for us.

8. The entrance of sin into the world, the incarnation of Christ, regeneration, the resurrection, and many other subject presented in the Bible are mysteries too deep for the human mind to comprehend.

9. In the natural world we are constantly surrounded with mysteries that we cannot fathom. The human body, astronauts in space - space exploration.

   Computers, the human body.

STUDY GUIDE ANSWERS 13 - WHAT TO DO WITH DOUBT

10. The very humblest form of life present a problem that the wisest of philosophers is powerless to explain. Everywhere are wonders beyond our ken. Should we then be surprised to find that in the spiritual world also there are mysteries that we cannot fathom.

    The difficulty lies solely in the weakness and narrowness of the human mind.

11. No. God has given us in the Scriptures sufficient evidence of their divine character.

    No. In the world we live in, are mysteries that we cannot understand.

    The difficulty lies solely in the weakness and narrowness of the human mind. God has given us in the Scriptures sufficient evidence of their divine character, and we are not to doubt God's word because we cannot understand all the mysteries of His providence.

12. The very grandeur and mystery of the theme presented should inspire faith in it as the word of God.

    Yes! If it contained no account of God but that which we could easily comprehend; if His greatness and majesty could be grasped by finite minds, then the Bible would not bear the unmistakable credentials of divine authority. The very grandeur and mystery of the themes presented should inspire faith in it as the word of God.

    Yes! If His greatness and majesty could be grasped by finite minds, then the Bible would not bear the unmistakable credentials of divine authority.

13. It has astonished and charmed the most highly cultivated minds while it enabled the humblest and uncultured to discern the way of salvation.

    Thus the plan of redemption is laid open to us, so that every soul may see the steps he is to take in repentance toward God's appointed way; yet beneath these truths, so easily understood, lie mysteries that are the hiding of His glory.

14. Mysteries that overpower the mind in its research, yet inspire the sincere seeker for truth with reverence and faith. The more he searches the Bible, the deeper is his conviction that it is the Word of the living God.

    The human reason bows before the majesty of divine revelation.

    He will be inspired with deeper conviction that it is the Word of the living God.

15. That the finite mind is inadequate to grasp the Infinite. That man with his limited human knowledge cannot understand the purpose of omniscience.

16. Satan works to pervert the investigative power of the mind, so that men feel impatient and defeated if they cannot explain every portion of scripture to their satisfaction.

STUDY GUIDE ANSWERS 13 - WHAT TO DO WITH DOUBT

A certain pride is mingled with the consideration of Bible truth, so that men feel impatient and defeated if they cannot explain every portion of scripture to their satisfaction.

17. They are not, however, chargeable to God's word but to man's perversion of it.

    No. Satan.

    No. To man's perversion of the word of God.

18. There would be for them no further discovery of truth, no growth in knowledge no further development of mind or heart. God would no longer be supreme.

19. There is only one way in which this knowledge can be obtained. We can attain to an understanding of God's Word only through the illumination of that Spirit by which the Word was given.

20. The study of the Bible will strengthen and elevate the mind as no other study can.

21. Yet we are to beware of deifying reason which is subject to the weakness and infirmity of humanity.

    When we come to the Bible, reason must acknowledge an authority superior to itself; and the heart and intellect must bow to the great I AM.

22. As when we enter His presence.

23. When the word of God is opened without reverence and prayer; when the thoughts and affections are not fixed upon God, or in harmony with His will, the mind is clouded with doubts; and in the very study of the Bible, skepticism strengthens.

24. Whenever men are not in word and deed seeking to be in harmony with God, then, however learned they may be, they are liable to err in their understanding of Scripture. It is not safe to trust their explanations.

25. The real cause of doubt and skepticism in most cases is the love of sin.

26. The teaching and restriction of God's Word are not welcomed to the proud sin loving, heart, and those who are unwilling to obey its requirements, and are ready to doubt its authority.

27. In order to arrive at truth we must have (1) a sincere desire to know the truth and (2) a willingness of heart to obey it.

28. 1. To obey the light, knowledge, one already has. To believe, to be, to do what you already have received from God.

    2. To give heed to the light that you have, and you will have greater light.

STUDY GUIDE ANSWERS 13 - WHAT TO DO WITH DOUBT

29. The evidence of experience.

30. God invites us to prove for ourselves the reality of His word, the truth of His promises. He bids us taste and see that He is good.

    Claim God's promises for yourself and they will be fulfilled.

31. By faith we look to the hereafter and grasp the pledge of God for a growth of intellect.

    Look to the hereafter, and grasp the pledge of God. And rejoice that all which has perplexed us in the providences of God will then be made plain.

32. Now we see through a glass, darkly, but then face to face: now I know in part; but then shall I know even as also I am known. 1 Corinthians 13:12. In heaven and the earth made new.

TEACH Services, Inc.
P U B L I S H I N G

We invite you to view the complete
selection of titles we publish at:
www.TEACHServices.com

We encourage you to write us
with your thoughts about this,
or any other book we publish at:
info@TEACHServices.com

TEACH Services' titles may be purchased in
bulk quantities for educational, fund-raising,
business, or promotional use.
bulksales@TEACHServices.com

Finally, if you are interested in seeing
your own book in print, please contact us at:
publishing@TEACHServices.com
We are happy to review your manuscript at no charge.

www.ingramcontent.com/pod-product-compliance
Lightning Source LLC
Chambersburg PA
CBHW081923170426
43200CB00014B/2813